Civil War

ghosts

of South Carolina

Civil War

ghosts

of South Carolina

Tally Johnson
TALLY JOHNSON 12/20

PROSPECTIVE PRESS
Winston-Salem

P ROSPECTIVE   P RESS   LLC

1959 Peace Haven Rd, #246, Winston-Salem, NC 27106 U.S.A.
www.prospectivepress.com

Published in the United States of America by PROSPECTIVE PRESS LLC

↑ TRADEMARK

CIVIL WAR GHOSTS OF SOUTH CAROLINA

ISBN 978-1-943419-06-7

First PROSPECTIVE PRESS trade paperback edition

Printed in the United States of America
First printing, October, 2020

Originally published in 2013 as *Civil War Ghosts of South Carolina*

The text of this book was typeset in Garamond

Dedication

This book is dedicated to the memory of my baby brother, Brennan Charles Wilson Johnson.

I would also like to thank my wife Rachel Wylie Johnson and my friends and family for their support and patience over the course of writing of this book and my others as well.

Contents

Brief Overview of the Civil War in South Carolina

Historians have disputed the root causes of the Civil War since the day after South Carolina left the Union in 1860. Some claim the seed for disunion was planted as early as 1619 when the first African-American slaves were shipped to Jamestown Virginia. Others move the date up to the Constitutional Convention of 1787 and the compromises that produced that document, such as the three/fifths compromise concerning counting slaves for purposes of representation, the bicameral legislature (one house with equal representation and the other divided by population), and the ending of the Atlantic slave trade by 1808. Ironically, given the views it would develop by the 1850s, South Carolina outlawed the interstate slave trade for a few years starting in 1792. Personally, I date the beginning of the end of the "old Union" from 1798 when Jefferson and Madison introduced the Virginia and Kentucky Resolutions in response to the Alien and Sedition Acts and opened the Pandora's Box of nullification and interposition. The resolutions argued that the states had the right and the duty to declare unconstitutional any acts of Congress that were not authorized by the Constitution. Adherents argue that the states can judge the constitutionality of central government laws and decrees.

The Kentucky Resolutions of 1798 argued that each individual state has the power to declare that federal laws are unconstitutional and void. The Kentucky Resolution of 1799 added that when the states determine that a law is unconstitutional, nullification by the states is the proper remedy. The Virginia Resolutions of 1798 refer to interposition: to express the idea that the states have a right to "interpose" to prevent harm caused by unconstitutional laws. The Virginia Resolutions contemplate joint action by the states. Here we find the seed that would grow and thrive in the brilliant mind of John C. Calhoun and be carefully cared for by Robert Barnwell Rhett and others. Secession became the answer of the South to every insult, every political setback, and every abolitionist provocation. South Carolina re-opened the Atlantic slave trade in 1803 but willingly ended it in 1808 per the Constitutional provision.

In 1820, pro-slavery sentiment begins to harden as the state made manumission of slaves illegal. This followed the organization of the American Colonization Society in 1816 meant to ease racial and slavery-related tensions by sending free blacks to the colony of Liberia in Africa. Southern support for the Society was based in large part on the belief that by removing free blacks from contact with slaves, escapes, revolts, and other agitation would decline, strengthening the slave system. Also in 1820, the possible admission of Missouri as a state put the balance between slave and free states in Congress in jeopardy. Luckily, a compromise was soon reached allowing Missouri in as a slave state, but with slavery excluded from future states north of her southern border but protected below and by bringing Maine in as a free state to maintain the balance. This pattern of joint admission would basically hold until the end of the Mexican War. In May 1822, the Denmark Vesey slave uprising broke out and was harshly put down. In the heightened state of concern following the abortive rising, South Carolina passed the Negro Seaman's Act in December 1822 which jailed free black sailors while their ship was in port in Charleston or other SC ports. Early in the life of the Act, the penalty for failure to pay for the cost of imprisonment was enslavement.

Starting in the mid-1820s, concern over Federal tariff policy and opposition to protection of Northern industry at the expense of Southern agriculture grew in South Carolina. I'm sure the elevation of Calhoun to the Vice-Presidency in 1825 and his ambition to become President had little to do with the agitation. Calhoun anonymously wrote the SC Exposition and Protest in response to the Tariff of Abominations of 1828, advocating nullification as a proper response to Constitutional disputes between state and federal governments hearkening back to the Virginia and Kentucky Resolutions. Ironically, Calhoun and his allies had designed the 1828 Tariff to be unpalatable to all sections in order to boost the electoral prospects of Andrew Jackson and Calhoun himself. After the tariff bill passed, Calhoun expected Jackson to push for lower rates immediately. When he did not, a rift began to form between the two native sons of South Carolina. By 1832, the split was open and complete. Calhoun resigned as Vice President to fight for Southern interests in the US Senate on December 18, 1832. On July 14, 1832, Jackson signed into law the Tariff of 1832. This compromise tariff received the support of most northerners and half of the southerners in Congress. The reductions were too little for South Carolina, and in November 1832 a state convention declared that the tariffs of both 1828 and 1832 were unconstitutional and unenforceable in South Carolina after February 1, 1833. Military preparations to resist anticipated federal enforcement were initiated by the state. In late February both the Force Bill, authorizing the President to use military forces against South Carolina, and a new negotiated tariff satisfactory to South Carolina were passed by Congress. The South Carolina convention reconvened and repealed its Nullification Ordinance and the Force Bill on March 11, 1833. A crisis had been averted, but the issues were left unresolved. The extension of slavery in to the West and the growing conflicts between radicals on both sides of the slavery issue would soon overshadow disputes of tariff rates for a generation or more. The fiery rhetoric of abolitionists like William Lloyd Garrison would soon be answered in kind by men like James Henry Hammond, Preston Brooks, and Robert Hayne.

In 1834, South Carolina made teaching slaves and free blacks to read illegal. In July 1835, a shipment of abolitionist mail was seized by a mob in Charleston and burnt. This incident led Postmaster General Amos Kendall to advise against delivering abolitionist tracts via the US Mail in the South, which policy is followed until the late 1850s. Not content to limit what slaveowners could do with their property only inside the state's border, the State Legislature made leaving the state with slaves with the intent of manumitting them illegal. In 1844, the Bluffton Movement tried to justify either "separate state action" towards secession or a vague guarantee of more safeguards for Southerners inside the Union after Calhoun was roundly defeated in a bid for the Democratic presidential nomination and the passage of the Tariff of 1842 was passed. Only Calhoun's open repudiation of the Movement stalled it, though it did position Robert Barnwell Rhett as Calhoun's logical successor as the theorist for the South.

The annexation of Texas in 1845 reopened dormant concerns over the role of slavery in the territories and in the role of the central government to police it. The Mexican War was fought between 1846 and 1848 with the future of slavery in any newly acquired territory being a major issue. In 1847, in response to the introduction of the failed Wilmot Proviso proposing to ban slavery from any land acquired from Mexico, Calhoun introduced resolutions giving the Southern view of the situation in the US Senate as follows: territories belonged to the states, not the federal government, all states had full access to all territories, the only condition Congress could require for statehood were that states have a republican form of government and meet all Constitutional requirements as to population, and Congress was barred by the Constitution from interfering with slavery. Remember, Calhoun had been a staunch nationalist in 1820 during the Missouri Crisis. No action was taken on these resolutions, but they stated the Southern view as well as could be done and remained the touchstone of the pro-slavery leaders up to 1860. Later, in early March 1850, in his last speech (which he was too ill to read) to the senate, Calhoun demands passage of a constitutional amendment giving the South the means to protect itself within the Union, especially by the creation of a two man presidency (one Northern and one Southern) both with an absolute veto as explained in his book Discourse on the Constitution and Government of the United States. Calhoun died on March 31, 1850, the demand remaining that his supporters reject any compromise. In June 1850, the Nashville Convention was convened in order to plan a united Southern response to any move towards banning slavery in the territories. It rejected calls for secession and instead issued a call for the extension of Missouri Compromise line to the Pacific, while rejecting the compromise proposed by Henry Clay. In November 1850, following the passage and signing of the Compromise measures proposed by Clay two months earlier, the Nashville Convention reconvened and advocated informally for secession and backed separate state action on that front. The rhetoric used in Nashville in November 1850 would be heard again and again over the next decade. The Compromise was a mixed bag; allowing California into the Union as a free state, Texas gave up claims on New Mexico and allowed the US Government to take up its debt; the slave trade was banned from Washington DC, although slavery remained legal and the Fugitive Slave Law was strengthened. The Compromise also saw the emergence of Stephen Douglas as a leading National Democrat and the emergence of the theory of popular sovereignty as a way to sidestep the slavery issue in the territories. In December of 1850, the South Carolina Legislature called for the election of two sets of delegates, one to a state convention and the other as delegates to a gathering of southern states to be held in Montgomery Alabama in January 1852; these delegates were also tasked with buying arms for the state militia. In February, immediate secessionists won a majority of the delegates to the state convention, and call for secession that May. However, cooperationists won a majority of the seats to the proposed Montgomery meeting, which was not held. To save face, the State Convention stated that the State had good cause to secede but declined to do so at that time.

In 1854, the Kansas-Nebraska Act blew the lid off of sectional discontent. By opening up all territories to popular sovereignty, the Act turned the Midwest into a rehearsal for civil war. Of course, South Carolina's politicians could not allow the fires to flicker before pouring extra fuel onto them. In May 1856, United States Representative Preston Brooks brutally beats US Senator Charles Sumner of Massachusetts on the floor of the US Senate after Sumner delivers a fiery anti-slavery speech on Kansas statehood with slavery, including perceived insults to US Senator from SC Andrew Butler (Brooks' uncle). Brooks' fellow Congressman from South Carolina, L.M. Keitt holds off those coming to aid Sumner with a pistol. On July 7, 1856, Brooks resigned from the US House and was unanimously re-elected by his district. Keitt was also overwhelmingly reelected within a month of resigning his seat in protest of the censure he received by the US House. The Dred Scott decision by the US Supreme Court in 1857 widened the gap between the sections by declaring that African-Americans are property and not people, declaring the Missouri Compromise unconstitutional, and by preventing Congress from imposing any limits on slavery in any territory. The futile attempt of John Brown to inspire a region-wide slave uprising in 1859 only inflamed matters and solidified Southerners towards secession as the best protection for slavery. Tensions would continue to build until the presidential election offered the South an out: the probable election of a member of the openly free-soil and anti-expansion of slavery Republican party as President.

In 1860, only the Democratic Party was a viable national party. The Whigs had faded away into history after 1850; the American Party (Know-Nothings) were weakening and beginning to split along sectional lines, and the Republican Party had no presence in the South at all except as a bogeyman used to inspire party loyalty. In April 1860, the Democratic National Convention opened in Charleston. When the majority report on the platform (which is strongly pro-southern) was rejected, southern delegates walked out after five days without nominating a candidate. In

June, both halves of the party reconvened in Baltimore at separate sites following another defeat for the South on the platform. The Northern Wing nominated US Senator Stephen Douglas of Illinois and the Southern Wing selected Vice President John Breckenridge of Kentucky. With this spilt, the election of the Republican nominee, Abraham Lincoln of Illinois, was practically guaranteed and with it secession. Breckenridge received all of South Carolina's electoral votes in December. However, some Federal officeholders did not wait for final tallies to make their decisions. On November 7, 1860, the Federal District Judge for South Carolina, Andrew Magrath, resigned his commission via a rousing speech from the bench, upon hearing of Lincoln's likely election as President. Magrath, in a nice piece of symmetry, would later serve as the last Confederate Governor of South Carolina. On the 10th, US Senator James Chestnut Junior resigned his seat and returned home to South Carolina. In December 1860, Francis Pickens was elected Governor and immediately asked the Federal Government to evacuate Fort Sumter. In that same month, the State Secession Convention convened in Columbia and immediately moved to friendlier ground in Charleston due to a smallpox outbreak in the state capital.On December 20, 1860 the State Convention passed unanimously the Ordinance of Secession, followed on Christmas Eve by the passage of the Declaration of Immediate Causes. From December 20, 1860 to February 8, 1861, SC is technically an independent republic.

On December 26, 1860, US Army Major Robert Anderson moved his troops from Fort Moultrie to Fort Sumter, without orders to do so. The next day South Carolina troops took over Fort Moultrie and Castle Pinckney. On December 28, a SC delegation in Washington demanded the removal of all US troops from Charleston and was refused on New Years Eve; on the previous day, SC troops seized the US Arsenal in Charleston. In early January 1861, fire from SC positions led to the withdrawal of the steamer Star of the West before it could resupply the Federal forces at Fort Sumter. On February 8, 1861 at Montgomery AL,

Firing on Fort Sumter, April 1861 — The long bloody conflict began here. After a night's bombardment, no casualties resulted. The rest of the war would prove to be far different.

the delegates from the seceding states passed the Provisional Constitution of the Confederate States of America. The next day, former Senator Jefferson Davis was elected Provisional President over Robert Barnwell Rhett, among other contenders.

April 12, 1861, Confederate troops under the command of General PGT Beauregard opened fire on Fort Sumter at 4:30 AM after Major Anderson rejected a final surrender demand from General James Chestnut Junior. The fort surrendered the next day with the only loss of life occurring during the surrender ceremony. On November 7 1861, Union Flag Officer Samuel Du Pont captured Port Royal and Forts Beauregard and Walker after a four-hour fight, taking Hilton Head Island and Beaufort shortly thereafter. This defeat led to the reconvening of the Secession Convention, which set up a Council to help manage the war effort alongside the Governor.

In May 1862, Robert Smalls, a slave serving as a harbor pilot turned the CSA Planter, a dispatch boat and transport, over to the blockading Union fleet, freeing himself and his family. The Battle of James Is-land-Battle of Secessionville (or the First Battle of James Island) was fought on June 16, 1862, resulting in a Confederate victory. The Battle of Simmons's Bluff was fought on June 21, 1862 near Meggett, south of Charleston. The battle resulted in the abandonment of Union attempts to seize the rail line leading from Savannah to Charleston. In August 1862, the United States War Department allowed the enlistment of for-mer slaves into the Union army in occupied South Carolina. This led to the formation of the first black regiment in US Army, the First Regiment of SC Volunteers in November. Colonel Thomas W. Higginson is named commander. Over five thousand Black men eventually joined the Union army from SC. In December, Brigadier General Milledge Bonham was elected Governor. The Secession Convention finally adjourned and the Legislature disbanded and annulled most acts of the Council.

In March 1863, General David Hunter seized Cole's and Folly Islands near Charleston for the Union Army and began to plan assaults on the city. On April 7, 1863, the recently promoted to Rear Admiral Samuel du Pont attacked Fort Sumter with a Union fleet, but was forced to retreat. This defeat is known as the First Battle of Charleston Harbor. On June 1, 1863, the Federal forces in Hilton Head launched a recruiting expe-dition for African-American units from Lowcountry plantations along the Combahee River. The force consisted of a portion of an artillery unit, three hundred soldiers of the 2nd South Carolina Volunteers, and a unit composed of former slaves who had enlisted in the Union army. The troops embarked in three vessels. The Federal force faced little re-sistance from the disorganized and surprised Confederates in the area. By the end of the raid, the Federal troops freed 725 slaves and burned plantation homes, mills, and a variety of agricultural stores. The Com-bahee Raid was mainly notable for the involvement of Moses herself, Harriet Tubman. The Second Battle of Charleston Harbor, also known as the Siege of Charleston Harbor, Siege of Fort Wagner, or Battle of Morris Island raged from July 19, 1863, to September 7, 1863. On July

Charleston 1865 — As the site of the start of the war, Charleston took a beating.

16, two feints were ordered by Union General Quincy Gillmore. One was directed towards James Island and was the inconclusive skirmish at Grimball's Landing. The other was a demonstration to threaten the Stono River railroad bridge. Neither feint was very effective. On July 19, 1863, General Gillmore attacked Battery Wagner on the northern tip of Morris Island with support from a fleet commanded by Rear Admiral John Dahlgren, but the assaults were twice repulsed, leading to a siege that lasted until September. In August 1863, using ships in the harbor and guns placed on Morris Island, Gillmore launched a bombardment of both Charleston and Fort Sumter lasting most of the month. Battery Wagner fell on September 7, but Sumter repulsed another attack on the ninth of the month. In October, the CSS David, a steam-powered semisubmersible torpedoed and sank the ironclad USS New Ironsides in Charleston Harbor.

Continuing Confederate successes under the waves on February 17, 1864, the hand-propelled submarine CSS Hunley sank the USS Housatonic in Charleston Harbor, but the Hunley also sank with a total loss of her crew of eight. On May 26, 1864, a planned attempt by the Union Army to cut the Charleston and Savannah Railroad bridges over the Ashepoo and South Edisto Rivers failed when two ships missed a rendezvous point, allowing the Confederates at Chapman's Fort to be reinforced, resulting in the loss of one vessel and bringing an end to attempts on the bridges. On November 30, the Battle of Honey Hill was fought in present day Jasper County. It was another unsuccessful Union attempt to cut the Charleston and Savannah railroad, this time near Pocotaligo. In December 1864, former US Judge Andrew Magrath was elected Governor. He served until May 25, 1865. On December 7 and 9, 1864, the entire Corps of Cadets of both the Citadel and Arsenal Military Academies were engaged in combat against Union troops at Tulifinny Creek near Yemassee. The Cadets forced the Union troops back to their lines and repulsed a counterattack. General Samuel Jones, CSA, commended the entire Corps for gallantry under fire. The Citadel is one of a select few colleges in the nation to have received a battle streamer for wartime service and the only one to have received multiple awards, of which Tulifinny is one.

On January 15, 1865, Major General William T. Sherman issued Field Order 15, giving the freed slaves possession of the Sea Islands from Charleston to the St. Johns River in Florida and all abandoned rice fields thirty miles inland as well. Sherman entered South Carolina on the 19th with sixty-five thousand men. The only real attempt to slow Sherman's advance through the state occurred at River's Bridge at the

Burning of Columbia 1865 — The capital of South Carolina was a natural target of the ire of Sherman's troops. However, most historians think the fire was accidental.

Salkehatchie River on February 3, 1865. About twelve hundred Confederates, behind strong entrenchments, sought to delay an entire wing of the Union Army and delayed its advance for a day. By the 16th, Columbia had surrendered after a brief bombardment from the Lexington side of the Congaree River, but burned the next night. Blame for the blaze was disputed for decades. On February 18, 1865, the Confederate Army abandoned Charleston and Fort Sumter. By mid-March, Sherman had left South Carolina, leaving behind destruction only rivaled by that suffered by Georgia. April 1865 opened with a Confederate defeat at Five Forks, Virginia, followed by the fall of both Petersburg and Richmond by the 4th. Confederate Jefferson Davis fled south, reaching South Carolina about April 26th. His wife Varina was in Chester, South Carolina by the 14th and in Abbeville by the 19th. On Easter Sunday, the 9th of April, Confederate General Robert E. Lee surrendered to Union General Ulysses S. Grant at Appomattox Court House. In mid-April, Felix De-Fontaine, a newspaper editor turned refugee managed to save both the Provisional and Permanent Confederate Constitutions along with other government records from looting refugees from Columbia in Chester, South Carolina. During his flight towards the Southwest, Jefferson Davis and his Cabinet stopped in several places in South Carolina. The first was Fort Mill, South Carolina in York County. Davis stayed at the home of Colonel Andrew Springs on the night of April 26th. Here, he accepted the resignation of George Trenholm of South Carolina as Secretary of the Treasury and appointed Postmaster General John Reagan of Texas to succeed Trenholm the next morning. The next night was spent at the home of Dr. James Bratton in Yorkville (now York). We will encounter Doctor Bratton again. The last Confederate Council of War was held in Abbeville South Carolina on May 2, 1865. President Davis met with Secretary of War Breckenridge, General Braxton Bragg, and and five other generals. All advised Davis to try to escape to the Southwest. Jefferson Davis was captured in Irwinville, Georgia on May 10, 1865. By April 26, Confederate General Joseph Johnston had surrendered all troops from North Carolina to Florida to Union General William T. Sherman. From April 5 to April 21, 1865, the Pee Dee region of South Carolina was the target of one last Union raid. General Edward Potter led this one and his target was the railroads, rolling stock, and military supplies gathered in the area near Sumter and Camden. This raid was marked by three different battles: Dingles Mill on April 9th, Boykins Mill on the 18th, and Dinkins Mill on the 19th. The skirmish at Boykins Mill was the site of the last Union officer killed in action, Lieutenant E.L. Stevens. The final military clash in South Carolina took place at Williamston when a group of cadets from the Arsenal military academy in Columbia encountered a group of stragglers from Stoneman's Raid. This encounter is also known as the Battle of Anderson. On May 25, 1865, Union General Quincy Gillmore deposed and arrested Governor Magrath, leading to the military rule and occupation of the state during the first part of Reconstruction. Federal troops would remain in the state until 1877. South Carolina lost 12,922 men to the war, twenty-three percent of its male white population of fighting age, and the highest percentage of any state in the nation.

Upcountry Region

Springwood Cemetery, Greenville's City of the Dead

Springwood Cemetery on Main Street in Greenville dates from 1812, although the land was not deeded for use as a graveyard until 1829. The person responsible for the first burial on what is now the site of Springwood was Chancellor Waddy Thompson, Senior, and the interment was that of his mother-in-law. If I may be permitted a brief digression, the Thompson family has a tie to two major incidents in American history. The first was the first attempted assassination of an American President, the confrontation of President Andrew Jackson (a native South Carolinian) and Richard Lawrence following the funeral of US Representative Warren Davis of South Carolina in 1835. Lawrence's pistols misfired, saving America the trauma of a Presidential assassination for another thirty years. Waddy Thompson, Junior succeeded Davis in Congress. The second was the confrontation of Andrew Jackson and the Bell Witch, one of America's best-known ghost legends (though not mentioned in any of Jackson's surviving papers) by way of the connection mentioned above. This confrontation of future President and the paranormal would be unequalled until the revelation that Jimmy Carter and others had witnessed an UFO in 1969 in Leary, Georgia. However, back to Springwood Cemetery. The Confederate Monument at Springwood was re-dedicated in 1924 on-site after being located downtown since 1892. The cemetery is the burial site of over two hundred Confederates, the identity of eighty known but only to God. Sightings and other incidents in Springwood include orbs, streaks of light, faces, and full figures seen in the wrought iron fencing around some graves near Elford Street. I doubt any of these sightings can be blamed on deceased Confederates due to its location in the cemetery, but anything could happen. Reports of figures of children of both sexes and a wounded solider (sadly, none of the sources mention which war) have been seen, especially by other children. In 2012, my brother-in-law Justin and I visited Springwood one sunny and breezy afternoon. There was no foot traffic in the area but the two of us, though cars zoomed past on all sides. As is so often the case, as soon as we entered the cemetery via the ornate main gate, a sense of calm descended and the bustle of 21st Century America faded. I thought I heard the low fading murmur of voices, like I had entered a room unannounced and uninvited near the Confederate Monument, but I am willing write that off as a combination of the locale and my mindset at the time. Notwithstanding the reputed haunting, Springwood is a historic site well worth the visit during operating hours, but don't disturb the grave markers or any funerals, since it is still an active cemetery.

Three Bridges Road near Powdersville

Supposedly, there was a Confederate ammunition dump at Powdersville near the old Opera House, but I have not found any verification. Powdersville is not included in Palmetto Place Names, which was complied by the WPA in the 1940s. Also unconfirmed is the story of a slave girl named Eloise, killed there along with her master by Union troops while the duo was en route to a battle. Her spirit has been seen along the road, and passersby have claimed to hear her dying screams. Anderson County was home to a Confederate Commissary depot and was the site of a skirmish in May, 1865, and this could be the source of this tale. I have driven through Powdersville several times and have not noticed anything unusual. In fact, a friend and I passed through Powdersville and rode the length of Three Bridges Road this spring and saw nothing, and yes, we were looking. If only there was more detail given as to the location of the murder…

Moonville Cemetery

Moonville is a community off US Highway 276 (Laurens Road) in the southeast corner of Greenville County. A Civil War cemetery is rumored to be just off US 276, on a dirt path to the right. If you go through the area at night, you will hear screams, loud breathing, the beating of drums, and other strange noises. No apparitions have been reported. The site is not visible from the highway, and I'm not a fan of riding down dirt paths in the country at night without permission. I have not experienced anything here, but eagerly awaiting hearing from anyone who has.

Wofford College

Wofford College is home to three different ghosts, two of which have ties to the Civil War era. The college was founded in 1859 by the United Methodist Church. The first haunting can be found in the auditorium in the Old Main Building, which is both the focal point of and the oldest building on campus. I discovered this occurrence, known to students as "Ole Green Eyes," during my senior year, with my good friend Phillip Stone, who is now the archivist at Wofford. Now, before you get overly excited, this version of "Ole Green Eyes" is nothing like his namesake from the battlefield at Chickamauga in Georgia. That version has two very different appearances. The most common one is that he appears as a headless Confederate soldier who roams the battlefield in search of his missing head. The more… outlandish… version is described as a

Wofford College campus, Spartanburg SC — Established in 1854, the Old Main building on campus served as a hospital, it and several other buildings on campus are haunted.

ghoul with orange-green eyes, wearing a cape that is largely hidden by its waist-length hair. This version is blamed for two different car accidents in the 1970s. Now, back to our tale, We entered the auditorium one night during our last semester on campus. We had been told that during the Civil War, Old Main served as a hospital for the Confederacy. According to the legend, a Yankee prisoner of war died at Old Main toward the end of the war and vowed to return to the scene of his death every year. The date of his return varies depending who you talk to, but we had been told that early March was our best bet to see anything unusual. We were told to keep an eye on the top edge of the drapes over the large windows on the outer wall. Sure enough, about halfway back from the stage, we saw two small green lights appear in space. My first reaction was to open the drapes and look for another light source or a prankster. Nothing was visible but the bulk of the library next door and the two small lights were still there, despite the additional light. We hung around for a few more minutes and the two spots remained visible as we left.

The other reputed haunting with Civil War ties at Wofford is found in the Carlisle-Wallace House, home of the dean of the college. This building dates to the Civil War and served as part of the hospital on the campus. Two Confederate soldiers died of smallpox in the house. People have reported hearing footsteps upstairs at night—despite there being no one upstairs—as well as other noises. According to campus lore, the haunting is explained by the desire of the dead soldiers to return to duty. I asked Phillip if, as the college archivist, he had come across any firsthand accounts or other information on these hauntings and he said no to both requests.

Rose Apartments (Former Rose Hotel), York

The Rose Hotel (now apartments) in York was built in 1852 by a man named William Edward Rose, not in honor of the white rose made famous by the Yorkists in the War of the Roses, which is the source of the name of the town. Mr. Rose was a Republican after the Civil War and his hotel was home to the officers under Major Lewis Merrill during the peak of Klan activity during Reconstruction. This may be the source of the sightings of uniformed men in both Union and Confederate uniforms in the hallways and on the staircases in the building. The sobbing of a woman has also been heard in an unidentified room. Other odd events reported include windows and doors opening and closing on their own, moving refrigerators, and toilets flushing themselves. The activity seems to have peaked right after a major renovation in the late 1990s and early 2000s. On a personal note, a friend of my wife Rachel and mine worked for the Yorkville Enquirer in the mid-2000s and lived in the Rose Apartments. Despite several visits, some lasting until the wee hours of the morning, I never saw anything unusual, but I did hear footsteps on the stairs one night after going outside to smoke. No one ever joined them as they rose to the top of the stairs. I merely nodded and knocked on her door for re-entry, knowing that no one would believe me.

A neighbor of the Rose Hotel and fellow Confederate veteran, Dr. Rufus Bratton, followed a different postwar path. He was one of the founders and leading lights of the Ku Klux Klan in York County and hosted Confederate President Jefferson Davis during Davis's flight from Richmond. Dr. Bratton was also behind the lynching of a black militiaman named Jim Williams at the Bratton homeplace in Brattonsville, now a living history farm and historic site. Bratton fled to Canada for a brief while after this incident. Visitors to Historic Brattonsville have reported seeing a black man stalking the grounds, looking intently for someone.

Architectural Drawing of Rose Hill Plantation, Union County, SC — Home of the "Secession Governor," William Henry Gist. The house and surrounding area are among several haunted hot spots in South Carolina.

Rose Hill

The area around Rose Hill State Park itself has its own share of legends. These tales are depicted in an October 24th, 2004 article from the Union Grapevine, a free newsletter. One story concerns mysterious lights that appear in the nearby woods just after dawn. Hunters claim that the light resembles a man on horseback carrying a lantern. Those who have seen the light believe it is Governor Gist, still making his morning rounds. Since legend has it that his horse was buried next to him, it is possible that this figure is him and I can believe that he would still be interested in the state of affairs at his former home.

There is another story concerning the Gist family and the area around Rose Hill. Prior to the Civil War, one of Governor's Gist's daughters and a slave companion were out berry picking near what is now Sardis

Road. A carriage came along and, for whatever reason, the horses were spooked. The daughter dove into the woods unharmed, but the slave girl was killed. Drivers along that road have reported seeing the two girls along the roadside, then witnessing the white child dive into the woods while the Black girl vanishes. Other stories concerning the area around Rose Hill include the troop of Confederate cavalry that has been seen on the road leading past the main house and in the surrounding woods, but only heard on the gravel drive in front of the house and never seen. During a visit to take pictures for this book, my brother-in-law and I took some photos of the exterior of the main house and inside the reconstructed outbuildings. In the outdoor kitchen, he reported the "face-finder" on his digital camera kept zooming in at a spot in the lower right of the photo just above the floor. Nothing appeared on any of the four shots he took, not even an orb. Just another day chasing ghosts…

Newberry College

The Lutheran Church established Newberry College in 1856. During the Civil War, the college was used as a Confederate hospital and, immediately after the war, as a US Army garrison. The college relocated to Walhalla in Oconee County from 1868 to 1877, returning with the end of Republican rule. In fact, the best-known ghost story on the campus dates back to the period of its use as a hospital and garrison.

Before the Civil War, a young man named John from Wisconsin fell in love with a local belle named Madeline. With the coming of conflict, John returned north to fight, while Madeline stayed in Newberry to roll bandages for the Confederacy. When the US Army took over the campus following the war, John returned to Newberry with his unit. Madeline hoped they would rekindle their affair and John encouraged this hope. However, in 1877, John left Newberry with his unit without even a farewell for Madeline. Madeline climbed the belfry tower in Keller Hall in hopes to catch John's attention as he rode past. However, failing to get any response, either the bell rope accidentally wrapped around her neck in the breeze and she slipped or she hung herself in despair. As she fell, the bell rang out. When a doctor examined her body, he determined that the fall was not lethal or that her neck was not broken. The official cause of death was listed as a broken heart. After students returned to the campus in 1877, the bell in Keller Hall would ring out one time every autumn without the help of human hands. After co-education arrived at Newberry in the 1920s, an enterprising male student started the tradition known as Madeline's return. A male student would ring the bell in Keller Hall, shouting "Don't fall in love with a Yankee!" while running to Smeltzer Hall, which was the female dormitory. In a 1986 article, the return of this tradition was rumored, despite the removal of the bell from Keller Hall to a trailer on campus.

Cry Baby Bridge

Yes, here's another version of a crybaby bridge. This version dates back to the end of the Civil War, after the burning of Columbia, when General Sherman was a terror. A group of refugees from the Columbia area heard a rumor that Sherman was coming and would burn all the towns and railroad bridges. Sadly, Sherman veered to the east and only an occasional patrol came through the area. Of course, in wartime, rumors are as true as facts and these exhausted folks fled north toward Spartanburg. They decided to hide under the railroad trestle over the Enoree River. A young mother and her baby were with the refugee party. In order to avoid attention from the approaching troops (though as it turned out, there were none), the mother kept her hand over the baby's mouth to keep it from crying. By morning, the baby had suffocated. The party tried to bury the child and move on, but the mother lost her mind and refused to allow anyone near her baby. The party continued on, only to look back and watch the mother leap from the trestle to the river below with her child in her arms. When the refugees reached the riverbank, only the lifeless child could be found floating in the current.

Today, as legend has it, if you walk across the trestle or the nearby highway bridge, a woman in an old-fashioned dress may join you. You may also be able to hear the soft, muffled cries of a baby. One day in March 2005, I decided to check this story out for myself. US Highway 221 goes over the Enoree, right next to a railway trestle, and that is the bridge I chose to explore. I arrived at the bridge about eight o'clock that night. Thankfully, traffic was non-existent and I decided to walk across, making as much noise as possible. I got about halfway over before I heard the soft sobbing of a child. I must confess, having expected to hear nothing, I panicked and sprinted back to my car. A few Johnny Cash songs later, I decided to walk up to the tracks and see if I could stir up the mother as well. I decided to chance it, but did not want to tarry, as trains sometimes do run on time. After a quick glance to see the lay of the land, I took off, taking two crossties at the time. I quickly crossed the river and headed right back across. I saw or heard nothing unusual, thankfully. I doubt my heart could have taken it if I had. When I dropped back by the site late last year with my brother-in-law in tow, we got several photos of the site from all angles and we both crossed the trestle more than once. Sadly, we were unaccompanied by any young mothers and neither of us heard anything unusual, though my brother-in-law did mention that the place struck him as being creepy.

Andy Johnson

You may be familiar with the early life of President Andrew Johnson, but did you know he spent about eighteen months in Laurens South Carolina before moving on to fame in Tennessee? In about 1820, he owned a tailor shop on the town square. He could be considered the most famous entrepreneur who has owned a business in Laurens. He went on to become United States Senator (twice), elected and Military Governor (ranking as a Brigadier General) of Tennessee, Vice-President of the United States under President Abraham Lincoln, and upon Lincoln's assassination, the 17th President of the United States. His arrival in Laurens followed his escape from indentured servitude in Raleigh after the death of his father. Here he met his first love, but was rejected when he proposed. He later moved with his mother to Greeneville, Tennessee where he met his wife Eliza and entered politics. The best-known ghost story connected with the first President Johnson involves his birthplace at Mordecai Manor in Raleigh, North Carolina. The light of a single candle has been seen in the windows of his birthplace. There is no electricity connected inside the house. Local lore has attributed the candle to either Johnson's mother Mary or his father Jacob. Most think it is Jacob looking for his family since they left the area by 1827 after his accidental death by drowning in 1811. The Andrew Johnson birthplace shares a site with another haunted location, the Mordecai House. The ghost of Mary Willis Mordecai Turk, who has appeared in a gray early-nineteenth century dress or has merely been heard playing the piano in the drawing room, haunts the Mordecai House. The house was investigated by the crew of the Ghost Hunters television show. The cast got the history of the house wrong and to a man came down with food poisoning. Your humble author on that subject requires no further comment.

Bethabara Cemetery

Bethabara Baptist Church near Cross Hill, South Carolina has been in existence since 1794. The current building was built in 1881. It is home to one of the more unusual Civil War-era hauntings in the state and, to be as well known as it is, it is strangely lacking in details. According to several sources, an unnamed soldier that served in the Civil War is buried here. His cross glows about three times a year and the color changes several times before returning to the normal rust color. The above is the most common version of the tale, but I have found another in a single source. In his book Weird Carolinas, Roger Manley mentions a glowing, cast-iron cross to be found at the Old Ford Baptist Church cemetery which is supposedly located near Cross Hill as well. He even gives an inscription: "Precious in the sight of the Lord is the death of his saints." However, the only stone I can find in the area with this inscription is that of Waddie T. Brown, which is a marble stone at Bethabara. No mention is made of any churches in Laurens County named Old Ford in any records I have consulted. Sadly, I think Mr. Manley's source was incorrect and he took it at face value. I have not seen any of the stones at Bethabara glow during any of my three visits. Of course, I have little interest in hanging out in a graveyard in the dark, following the theory that since ghosts were once people and most folks don't hang out in graveyards at odd hours. Not to mention the fact that so many irresponsible "ghost-hunters" have desecrated graves and otherwise damaged markers that getting permission for a vigil at a graveyard, especially a rural one, is about as like as being invited to tour the vaults at Fort Knox, unguarded, with an empty backpack. The only Confederate marker I can find in my notes for another book was for a James L. Atchison who lived from 1841 to 1911. His Iron Cross is carved onto his gray and untarnished marble headstone. Now, there are over two hundred marked graves at Bethabara Baptist Church and this may not be "the one," but the stone was odd enough to catch my eye as a local historian and archivist. I have my doubts that any of the stones in this cemetery glow, but if you decide to investigate, please get permission and be respectful of the dead and their families. Future genealogists and historians will thank you, as will I.

Sleepy Hollow Lane

Sleepy Hollow Lane near Lockhart, on the Broad River and on the Union-Chester County line, has been rumored to be haunted by a one-armed figure in gray standing on the roadside, crying for help. Legends differ on how he came to be there. The first theory is that the man was killed in the Civil War, but there is no evidence of any deaths in the area during that period. The second theory came from one of my friend Susan Hoff Roddey's coworkers and a native of the area. She claims the man is a local eccentric who was prone to harass passing motorists after losing an arm in an industrial accident. I have driven through the area at night and have not seen anyone on the side of the road, with or without a missing arm, but I urge those interested to check it out for themselves.

Burrell Hemphill

One thing I found to be odd while working on this book was the dearth of ghost lore about the Civil War in my adopted home county of Chester. While the city has about a half-dozen haunted sites and the county itself has about that many, only one has a tie to the Civil War era. It serves as an excellent reminder that, although the politicians claimed the war was about slavery or state rights or some other higher purpose, some of those who fought were motivated by more… economic reasons. By the time Sherman's army had reached South Carolina, stories of the devastation wrought by his foragers or bummers, as their civilian victims knew them, were already legendary. The flames of Columbia in Sherman's wake only added to the foreboding of those close to his path north. The Hemphill family was among those concerned. Robert Hemphill, a kinsman of noted politicians in both Texas and South Carolina, fled north into North Carolina as Sherman neared Columbia, leaving Burrell Hemphill, a possible relative and body servant to deal with the Federal

Sherman's Bummers — Much like in Georgia, these unofficial foragers struck terror into South Carolinians. Even a rumor of their approach sparked panic. Burrell Hemphill met his fate at the hands of men like these.v

foragers. Scholars believe Burrell knew the burial site of the family silver and that Robert Hemphill had fled with any actual money on site. The soldiers did not believe Burrell and dragged him a half mile to Hopewell Associate Reformed Presbyterian Church. After further questioning, Burrell was no more forthcoming as before, so the bummers hung him from a nearby black gum tree and riddled his corpse with bullets. A nearby cotton barn was burnt as well, with the loss of three hundred bales of cotton. A marker was placed in the churchyard recognizing Burrell's loyalty to his owner and his membership in the church.

My wife's family has an annual reunion at Hopewell ARP Church every summer. Over the years, I have had the opportunity to chat with most if not all of her cousins, aunts, and uncles. During one smoke-filled chat on the church porch, I asked about the marker honoring Burrell Hemphill's memory. I was told the story above and was also informed that a shadowy figure has been seen approaching the church door just before dusk on cold February evenings. Popular opinion is that the figure is Burrell Hemphill trying to find some safety. I hope he eventually finds it.

Midlands Region

Battle of Aiken

The Battle of Aiken was one of the few bits of good news to reach Confederate ears from the time when Sherman left Savannah until after the burning of Columbia. It was a classic cavalry battle that was fought to protect Augusta—one of the few river ports still usable by the Confederacy—and the cottons mill at Graniteville. Major General Judson Kilpatrick who had recently burned Barnwell before seizing and destroying the railroad tracks and several cars near Blackville commanded the Union cavalry. Kilpatrick was unpopular with civilians because he refused to control his bummers. Many complaints of rape and general ill treatment followed Kilpatrick through South Carolina. He was also known as "Kill-Cavalry" due to his poor tactics and lack of concern for the welfare of his men.

Joseph Wheeler, known as "Fighting Joe," who ranked just behind J.E.B. Stuart and Wade Hampton in his skills as a cavalry leader, led the Confederate cavalry. He was also young enough that some thirty plus years later, he served as a General in the American Army and was active on the frontlines during the Spanish-American War in 1898 and the Philippines Insurrection in 1900 while serving as a Congressman from Alabama. Wheeler decided to intercept Kilpatrick in Aiken on February 10, 1865. He set up an ambush in town and ordered his men to hold their fire until all of Kilpatrick's men were in range. Of course, a few troopers opened fire prematurely, springing the trap early. At the end of the melee, which featured hand-to-hand combat and flashing sabers, the Confederates held the field and had blunted Sherman's feint toward Augusta. General Kilpatrick fled the field ahead of a handful of Confederate troopers, losing his hat in his rush to escape. Union losses (killed, wounded and captured) were 495. Confederate losses (killed, wounded and captured) were 251. Of course, Sherman completely bypassed the Augusta area after the skirmish and pressed on to Columbia, Cheraw, and Bentonville.

On February 10–13 every year, the E. Porter Alexander Camp of the Sons of Confederate Veterans hosts a reenactment of the battle. The granite marker marking the site of the battle was dedicated on February 13, 1960 and was one of the first ceremonies marking the centennial of the Confederacy. One feature of this reenactment is a cavalry charge including a few riderless horses to honor the fallen. At the 1999 reenactment, a photojournalist documenting the scene took a photograph that shows a Confederate general, who was far from the field of battle in February 1865, riding one of the horses. According to an account published by Randall Floyd, noted Southern folklorist, when the photograph was developed General Robert E. Lee was seen on one of the riderless horses. Several experts examined the photograph and declared it genuine. Sadly, no reenactments since have been marked by any other ghostly activity. I have not been lucky enough to see the photograph or any reproductions of it. However, I seriously doubt that General Lee even gave any thought to the Battle of Aiken either at the time it occurred or in the remaining five years he lived afterward. I imagine he would have been more concerned with the immediate aftereffects of the fall of

Richmond and the approaching Union army under General Grant. The fact that General Lee does not reappear at his former home in Arlington, Virginia or at any other Civil War battlefield, like Gettysburg, Petersburg, or even Appomattox, leads me to believe that the general has found lasting peace. Also, most ghosts tend to have some connection to a site they return to, however fleeting. Though Lee did command the South Carolina Department after the fall of Port Royal briefly, his attention was focused on Charleston and the rest of the coast. I have found no tie between General Lee and the Aiken area. In Mr. Floyd's article on the photograph, he states that there is a strong resemblance to other well-known photos of General Lee on horseback as seen in works by noted Civil War scholars like Emory Thomas, which only gives credence to my personal theory that the photograph is an accidental double exposure. My one time witnessing the reenactment was an enjoyable and educational experience, but I have no unusual happenings to report.

Oak Grove Plantation

Despite the long history of settlement in the Hampton County area, I have managed to find very few stories to tell about the ghosts in the area. However, according to an owner of the house, the old Augusta Stage Coach Inn, better known in the area as Oak Grove Plantation or the Richardson place, is haunted. Several orbs have been reported in photographs taken in different rooms at different times. The orbs were all caught in motion and were of different sizes. None of the orbs were visible to the naked eye. To me, this implies actual ghostly activity more than the classic shots of static or yellowish globs of light. I feel that motion and a variety in sizes and colors signify at least remedial intelligence, whereas the motionless images imply merely a release of long built-up dust. The house was used by General Sherman as his headquarters during his well-known trip through the area in 1865 and is mentioned in his memoirs. This use of the house not only explains how the property escaped the torches of the bummers, but may also explain one feature of the reported haunting. Even though the main house burned in 2000 and has since been renovated, local lore still mentions sightings of Union soldiers staring out of windows, apparently still on guard duty, even when the house has been vacant. Other odd reports over the years include heavy footsteps on the main staircase, men's voices in quiet, indistinct conversation, and the various bangs, creaks, and bumps associated with old houses, even those that are not haunted. The current owners of the house claim not to have seen or heard anything out of the ordinary and remind potential visitors that the property is posted no hunting or trespassing and that it is private property; please respect their wishes. I have included the story simply due to the historic nature of the haunting.

Rivers Bridge

The Battle of Rivers Bridge was the first organized attempt by Confederate troops to slow Sherman's advance through southeastern Georgia and western South Carolina after the fall of Savannah and was the only major battle fought during Sherman's advance through the state. The battle, for all its import, is known by several names other than Rivers Bridge, including Duck Creek, Hickory Hill, Owens' Crossroads, Lawtonville, and Salkehatchie River. Confederate Major General Lafayette McLaws led about 1,200 well-fortified troops, who were blocking the crossing of the Salkehatchie River. Between the strong fortifications, trenches, and the heavy winter floods, McLaws felt secure and believed he could stall Sherman long enough for troops to rally behind him unless he were flanked. On February 3, 1865, the Union right wing under Major General Joseph A. Mower and Lieutenant General Giles A. Smith totaling some 28,000 troops, decided to either overwhelm or outflank the obstructing Confederates. Hasty bridges were thrown up in the face of fairly steady artillery fire. Most of the Union infantry had to wade through freezing, chest-deep waters. Two Union brigades flanked the Confederates on their right, and McLaws withdrew toward Branchville, abandoning the entire Salkehatchie line. Total casualties were about three hundred,

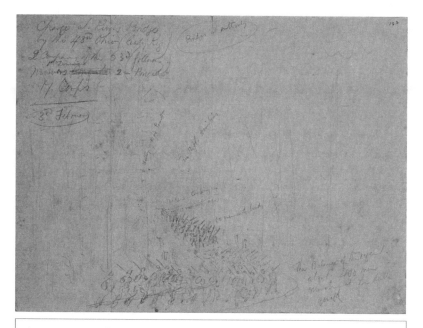

Charge at Rivers Bridge, Bamberg County, SC — Can a battle that took place in winter have ghostly echoes even in summer?

with the Confederates losing the majority. The entire affray lasted a few hours and delayed Sherman for about a day. As Sherman had predicted, if he could cross the Salkehatchie he could capture Columbia, which fell about two weeks later.

In August 2006, I visited Rivers Bridge State Historic Site while doing research for this book. I needed a break from driving, and the brochure for the park offered the promise of a one-and-a-half-mile interpretive trail. Since my real job concerned South Carolina history, I am ashamed to admit that this was my first visit to Rivers Bridge. I was aware of its role in the Civil War, but beyond that, I was simply after a few minutes of leg stretching. I paid the admission fee and took off down the trail. It took me a few minutes to get used to the quiet of the woods and surrounding marsh. Six hours of road noise and a very loud iPod didn't help to speed the transition. The markers were informative and the Confederate earthworks were well preserved. I arrived at the river, where the trail turned to the right after about ten minutes, and decided to just stand there and see if I could add any birds to my life list, such as it is, or see any other wildlife. Black water rivers are a rare sight in the rolling hills of my native Upcountry, and as I stood there looking across the river, a flash of blue caught my eye just above the water line in the trees of the marsh. Thankfully, I was alone, so I just stood still and quietly waited to see what it was. The blue moved out from behind a tree and I realized with a start that it was a dark-haired, bearded man in what appeared to be a blue wool jacket. He was carrying an old-fashioned rifle. I am not an expert on Civil War weapons, so forgive me if I plead ignorance as to what kind exactly it was. I thought about shouting a warning about swimming being prohibited, or even about snakes, but the shock of seeing him hit me like a shot. In amazement, I watched the figure, ignoring the steady buzz of feasting mosquitoes. When he thrust his arms out and fell backward into the murky water without a splash, the spell of the moment was broken. I was stunned to see anything out of the ordinary as no folklore is connected with the site. The fact that the battle was in February and my visit was in August also made the appearance of the apparition unexpected. I skipped the rest of the trail and decided to head back toward civilization. At the gate, I met a young couple from Tennessee who were Civil War buffs and working in the area. I explained the significance of the site to them briefly and headed toward Denmark. En route, I called my wife and told her about what I had seen. She humored me as wives often do their eccentric husbands.

Lucy Pickens

This story more properly belongs in Aiken County as that is where the house in question currently is located, but since the possible ghost lived and died in Edgefield, I'll tell it here. Lucy Holcombe Pickens was born in 1832 in Tennessee and grew up in Texas. She was so renowned a beauty that not even the Mississippi state legislature was immune to her, as that august body recessed in her honor. Her ties to South Carolina and Edgefield County began in 1858 when she met Colonel Francis W. Pickens, a member of a noted South Carolina family with ties to the "Wizard Owl" of the Revolution, Andrew Pickens, Sr. He was a former congressman who had just lost a bid for a U.S. Senate seat, but was being considered for a diplomatic post. He was also twenty-seven years her senior and twice widowed, but she agreed to marry him if he took the appointment as U.S. minister to Russia. He did so and they were married in April 1858. Their only daughter, Olga Pickens, was born at the Winter Palace in Saint Petersburg, Russia, and Tsar Alexander II and the Tsarina were the child's godparents. In fact, the tsar gave Olga a lifelong nickname, "Douschka," which meant "darling" in Russian. With the turmoil in the South rising to a fever pitch with the looming election of Republican Abraham Lincoln to the presidency, the Pickens family returned home in August 1860. The friendship between a Southern slave owner and the tsar who freed Russia's serfs is a historical fact that defies belief. As the saying goes, "there's a novel there somewhere."

After returning home, Francis Pickens was elected governor of South Carolina in December 1860, just three days before the state left the Union. He served as governor through the blockade of and the firing on Fort Sumter, which Lucy watched from a Charleston rooftop. He served until 1862. Lucy sold jewels given to her as a gift by the tsar to equip a Confederate unit, The Holcombe Legion, and was the only woman to appear on Confederate money, appearing on three issues of $100 bills and one issue of the $1 bill. She died at her home, Edgewood, in 1899 and was buried with her husband and daughter.

In 1929, Mrs. Eulalie Salley of Aiken bought Edgewood and decided to move it to Aiken, specifically to Kalmia Hill, where one of the earliest recorded appearances of the famed "Red Shirts" of the 1876 campaign to elect Wade Hampton III governor occurred. Mrs. Salley was a noted suffragist and was the first female realtor in South Carolina. Mrs. Salley was told at the time that Mrs. Pickens haunted her former home and would not take the move well. The guest room during the ownership of Mrs.

Salley was formerly Lucy Pickens's bedroom. Visitors reported smelling a strong perfume and hearing the swish of silk skirts and the rustle of petticoats when the lights were turned on. Other visitors reported the feeling of not being alone in the room or of being watched. Mrs. Salley never reported any odd events. The house is on the National Register of Historic Places and is privately owned. When I called to confirm the story, I was told in the strongest terms that the house was not haunted. I have included the story due to its historical interest. Please do not disturb the current owners.

Badwell Cemetery

Badwell Cemetery was the family burial grounds of first the Gibert family and later the Petigru family. Reverend Jean (or John) Louis Gibert was the leader of the French Huguenot settlement at New Bordeaux, which was established about 1764 in order to allow the Huguenots the freedom to worship as they saw fit and to escape the growing persecution of French Protestantism following the revocation of the Edict of Nantes. Currently, only one house remains from New Bordeaux, the Guillebeau House, which was built about 1770. Some of the settlers planted vines and produced the first commercial wine made in South Carolina.

James Petigru was the dominant anti-nullification and Unionist leader in South Carolina. His strong opposition to positions favored by the states-rights faction led by John C. Calhoun limited his office holding to one term in the South Carolina House of Representatives after 1830. Petigru was the lead counsel for the Unionists in the case of McCready v. Hunt, focusing on test oaths and States Rights, which was brought before the South Carolina Court of Appeals in 1834. The case involved a "test oath" passed by the South Carolina legislature in November 1832, requiring members of the state militia to pledge "faithful and true allegiance" to the State of South Carolina. The law was vague on the underlying and contentious issue of sovereignty, and did not specifically state whether allegiance to the state was superior to allegiance to the federal government. However, dispute over the oath immediately erupted. The "Nullifier" faction asserted that allegiance to the state had precedence over allegiance to the federal government, while "Unionists" asserted that the federal government had primacy over all states. The Unionists won the case, but lost the fight in the arenas of public opinion and state government. An amendment to the state Constitution was passed asserting the supremacy of allegiance to the state over the Union. Prior to these events, Petigru served as state attorney general for a term in 1822 before he split with Calhoun. Petigru may not have held a U.S. Senate seat or served as governor, but his role as a Unionist leader served to influence Unionist leaders like Benjamin Perry and James Orr. James Petigru was also the grandson of Reverend Jean Louis Gibert. Petigru also oversaw the codification of the laws of South Carolina and is best remembered for his quote, "South Carolina is too small for a republic and too large for an insane asylum." Uttered after secession, the quote is still used to describe politics in the state and has been applicable hundreds of times in the course of the last 150 years. Petigru did not expect South Carolina to ever re-join the Union, but died before the end of war proved him wrong on that point. Despite his family ties to Badwell Cemetery, he is buried at Saint Michael's Church in Charleston.

To my knowledge, neither of these distinguished gentlemen features in the haunting at Badwell Cemetery. The account I found online claims that a troll has been seen walking the perimeter just outside the stonewall! The gate (no longer on site) was iron and featured a life-size grim reaper. Many odd events have occurred, though the website does not give any details; however, I will mention one that occurred on my only visit.

I visited Badwell Cemetery on a whim after finding the account of the haunting online. The site has a state historical highway marker nearby, so it's easy to find, though only visit if you will treat the area with the respect the cemetery deserves. I arrived about 8: 00 PM on a Saturday evening several summers ago. After walking through the cemetery and transcribing a few of the stones, I was heading back to my car when I glanced back to make sure I had everything and saw three white lights flit through the trees, just above eye level. Now, I'm six feet and some change tall, so these lights were too high and large to be fireflies flying in formation. They passed through a gravestone and vanished—did not flicker out, did not break, just simply vanished as suddenly as they came. I nodded, kept walking to my car and continued home. Some things just defy explanation.

Blanding Street, Columbia

What I call "one-and-dones" are better known to students of ghost lore as crisis apparitions. Crisis apparitions are ghost that have minimal interaction with the living and usually appear to serve as a warning of future events or to protect a site from interference of one kind or another. Blanding Street is a major east-west route through downtown Columbia and has been the site of two such occurrences. The earliest recorded event was at the site of the former Christ Episcopal Church at the corner of Marion and Blanding Streets. The church burned in February 1865 along with much of Columbia's antebellum architecture. For several months after the fire, neighbors and passersby reported seeing "angels" gathering the shell of the chancel at the spot formerly occupied by the altar. I believe that the "angels" were returning Confederate veterans who meant for no further harm to come to the building. However, more sinister motives could be attributed to the figures, such as looters or other criminals taking advantage of the credulity of a beaten and demoralized populace. The church did not recover from this trauma and by 1870 the parish was defunct. I believe, the church's site is now a parking lot, but could one of the nearby houses.

The second appearance dates to the spring of 1914 and is much better documented than the angels at Christ Episcopal. The apparition of a phantom on horseback above the treetops appeared nightly for about a week and caused quite the sensation. The figure was seen to appear, and then the horse reared and took off on a journey of unknown purpose. Despite the detail visible in the figure, including the stitching on the saddle and reins, exactly who it was is still the source of some controversy. Contemporary accounts claim that it was one of the Four Horsemen of the Apocalypse or that it was former Confederate General Wade Hampton III. The appearance of Hampton was mentioned in connection with the start of World War I that autumn, as a forewarning of the bloodshed to come. To my ears, this sounds like a posthumous explanation that no one thought of at the time. Since General Hampton had been dead for twelve years at this point, I doubt he would be very concerned with the outbreak of a war in Europe. Sadly, I must write this off using the time-honored excuse of "mass hysteria." I think that once the word got out about the phantom horseman, the story grew from there and folks saw what they wanted to see. On a related note, the current Columbia Visitors Guide states that legend claims that the statue of General Hampton on horseback on the State House grounds comes to life and gallops around Columbia on certain nights. I doubt this, but the visual is interesting to say the least.

USC

The historic Horseshoe at the University of South Carolina is the haunt of a Columbia lady who was forced to serve as a nurse in one of the dorms after the Union occupation and burning of Columbia in 1865. She was raped, but forced by her destitute family to return. She gained revenge by poisoning the invalids in her care. Even now, she may appear to "Yankees" and offer them a glass of tea. Sadly, every building on campus that was extant at the time has been claimed as the site of this tragedy, and it has never been verified. Still, if a young beauty in period clothing offers you some tea while on campus and you hail from a state north of Kentucky or Maryland respectfully decline, just in case.

J. Rion McKissick, president of the University of South Carolina from 1936 until his death in 1944 is buried near the Horseshoe in front of

South Caroliniana Library, University of South Carolina Campus, Columbia SC — The campus was used as a hospital and was spared damage by the burning of Columbia, but echoes of the period linger.

the McKissick Museum. His ghost has been seen on the balcony of the South Carolinana Library and has been known to scatter books and papers all over the library. During the Bicentennial festivities in 1976, President McKissick and General Wade Hampton III were seen inside McKissack reading newspapers and faded away when spoken to, as they were in the building after hours. This sighting is noteworthy as the most recent sighting of Wade Hampton and the only one I have come across in which he was identified without any doubt, unlike the horseman seen on Blanding Street in 1914 mentioned above.

The Longstreet Theater located across Greene Street from the Horseshoe is home to two very different hauntings. The building is named after Augustus B. Longstreet, president of South Carolina College from 1857 to 1861 and uncle of Confederate General James Longstreet, who was born in Edgefield County, South Carolina and whom we will hear more from later. President Longstreet's tenure at South Carolina College ended when the entire student body enlisted as a group into the Confederate Army. The first haunting is focused on the basement of the building and dates from its use during the Civil War as a military hospital and morgue. Reports of lights going on and off by themselves, strange noises and smells, feelings of foreboding and of being watched, and sudden temperature drops have all been made over the years and blamed on one of the many Confederates who died on-site.

The second haunting is located in the now off-limits steam tunnels that run under the campus and dates back to the late 1940s and is one of the weirdest ghost tales I've heard in my career as an author and storyteller. It concerns the Third Eye Man. He was seen sliding into a manhole near Longstreet in 1949 and besides his extra eye was noticeable due to his being dressed solely in silver. His most recent appearance occurred in the late 1960s when a man matching his description reportedly assaulted some students in the tunnel near Gambrell Hall with a metal pipe. After this report, the tunnels were closed to access by students and all other unauthorized personnel, as I found out while working my last book, Ghosts of the Pee Dee.

The Statehouse and Grounds

The haunting of the statehouse grounds is localized near a ginkgo tree on the grounds. Some sources say that some of Sherman's soldiers are to blame for the pushes and shoves some have felt, while others say that Captain Lunsford may be responsible. Captain Swanson Lunsford was a native of Virginia who lived for several years in Columbia and died in 1799. He fought in the Revolution under "Light-Horse Harry" Lee, who was the father of Robert E. Lee. Captain Lunsford's grave was the only grave on the grounds of a state house in the United States until the burial of Huey Long on the grounds of the State House in Baton Rouge Louisiana in 1936. Lunsford's grave predates the siting of the State House, however.

South Carolina State House — Still bearing the scars of Sherman's bombardment, the seat of government of South Carolina is home to several ghosts.

But by far the better-known haunting at the statehouse is centered near the rotunda. According to legend, prior to major renovations in the 1960s, tourists and workers could access the underside of the dome more easily than currently. Either a workman or young student fell from the edge of the rotunda to the marble floor below, leaving an indelible bloodstain still present under the carpet there now. People have reported hearing a man's voice describing the fall and the sound of heavy running footsteps that echo like hard soles on marble, stories that lend more credence to the workman falling than the boy. I have visited both the grounds and statehouse itself numerous times and have not encountered either of these spirits. But I hold out hope, in echo of the state motto.

Hampton-Preston House

Ainsley Hall, a rich Columbia merchant, built what is now known as the Hampton-Preston House in 1818. A few years later, it was purchased by the first Wade Hampton. Both his son and grandson, each also named Wade

Hampton, lived in the house at times, though Wade Hampton I's daughter, Caroline Hampton Preston, and her husband actually owned it until 1865. During the occupation of Columbia by Union forces, it served as the headquarters for Major General John "Black Jack" Logan, whose ghost is supposed to haunt the former home of the U.S. Senate Military Affairs

Wade Hampton III — One of the South's best cavalry generals and later the Redeemer or Bourbon Governor of South Carolina and a US Senator, Hampton plays a role in a few of the ghostly legends of his home state.

Hampton-Preston Mansion, Columbia, SC — Home of the family of the best known South Carolina Civil War General and Bourbon statesman, Wade Hampton III; the house is the site of several hauntings.

Committee, of which he was chairman following the war. The home is on the National Register of Historic Places and is maintained by the Historic Columbia Foundation, which has run the house as a museum since 1970. Admission is charged and it is open to the public. No identity has been established for the ghost that has caused many malfunctions of audio and video recording equipment, candles that have been extinguished to relight, and is the source for loud moans and shaking chandeliers inside the house. Rocking chairs have rocked on their own. A gray-haired lady has been seen on the stairs. One report has her shaking her fist at a visitor wearing blue. Speculation claims this lady could be Caroline Hampton Preston, sister of Wade Hampton III. Children have been heard in the attic, which

Sherman on march through South Carolina — Sherman and his troops planned to make South Carolina suffer and his movements through the state led Confederate authorities to make panicked decisions.

is closed to visitors and seen in the windows by visitors on the grounds while the house was closed to guests. Glass globes have fallen from secure sconces and candles have gone missing from chandeliers. Feelings of being watched and reports of docents having their necks blown on or breathed on have also been reported. I have been to several meetings at the Hampton-Preston House, as well as taken the tour, and I have seen and heard nothing out of the ordinary. You may have better luck.

SC State Museum

The South Carolina State Museum is housed in the former Columbia Mills building which was the world's first totally electric-powered mill in the world when it opened in 1894. The Museum is located on the Congaree River within sight of where Sherman's troops opened fire on the city in February 1865. It is home to several ghosts including a headless man seen just prior to closing time for the Museum exiting the old freight elevator carrying his head in his hands. As he walks down the hall, he abruptly vanishes. The same elevator is the focal point for another haunting. A man has been seen entering the elevator and starting it, regardless of any waiting visitors. Even if the elevator is immediately recalled without reaching the floor, it is empty on arrival. A young African-American woman in dust-coated mourning clothes has been seen near the exhibit of a cooling board, used when funerals were held in the home. The most convincing haunting at the State Museum to my mind concerns my encounter with what I took to be a museum employee near the model of the Confederate submarine, the CSS Hunley. He was wearing denim overalls and was leaning on the rail next to the model, which overhangs the exhibit hall. I was visiting the museum with friends and was babysitting my god-daughter, who decided to trot ahead to look at some exhibit or another. I stopped to ask the man if he had seen a toddler go by when he turned and took a step towards the Hunley and vanished as he passed through the railing. After a few seconds my god-daughter walked up and asked what I was staring at. I shook my head and we moved on. I have visited the State Museum a dozen times since and have never had a similar experience, sadly. There have been reports since of a man wandering the exhibits overalls and heavy boots. He may be the same one that I saw, but some reports have named him "Bubba" and placed his hot spot on the third floor.

General Samuel McGowan, aka The Fifth Avenue Ghost

Samuel McGowan was born on October 9, 1819 in Laurens District, South Carolina. He graduated from South Carolina College and read law before being admitted to the bar. He was known for his speaking skills, and he was soon elected to the state legislature. He served in the Mexican War as a captain and was commended for his actions at the Battle of Chapultepec. Following the war, he returned to his law practice and rose to the rank of major general in the South Carolina militia.

His first action occurred as he commanded a brigade at the bombardment of Fort Sumter. He served on Brigadier General Milledge Luke

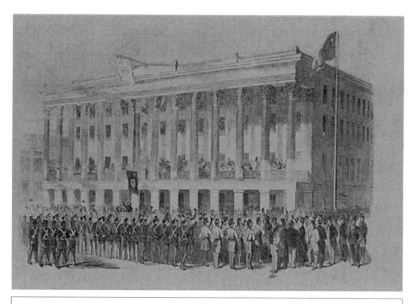

General Samuel McGowan addressing volunteers — General McGowan may have been a case of mistaken identity by the famed ghost hunter Hans Holzer.

Bonham's staff at the Battle of First Manassas. Following the fighting there, he was assigned to the 14th South Carolina Infantry where he rose to the rank of colonel. This regiment became a part of Maxcy Gregg's South Carolina brigade in the Army of Northern Virginia. They saw heavy fighting during the Seven Days battle's and McGowan was slightly wounded at Gaines' Mill, though he never left the field.

He was severely wounded at Second Manassas, which caused him to miss the Battle of Antietam (Sharpsburg). He would be back in command of his regiment at the Battle of Fredericksburg. Maxcy Gregg was mortally wounded during this battle and McGowan was promoted over two senior colonels to command the brigade. His promotion to brigadier general occurred on January 17, 1863. He wasn't a strict disciplinarian, but was a confident commander.

His first action as a brigadier general occurred at the Battle of Chancellorsville. Attacking a line of breastworks, his brigade was repulsed, but not before McGowan was struck below the knee by a bullet. He would be out of action until February of 1864, meaning he would miss Gettysburg. When he returned, he was forced to use a cane.

McGowan's South Carolina brigade was broken at the Battle of the Wilderness. He reformed his men in the rear and led them back to the fight. At Spotsylvania, his brigade helped save the Confederate Army when the "Mule Shoe" was overrun. He was struck in the right arm by a bullet during this attack and would not return to duty until the brigade was in the trenches of Petersburg. He would surrender with his men at Appomattox.

Following the war, he would eventually return to the state legislature and then serve as a judge on the state supreme court. He died in 1897 at the age of 77 and rests today in Long Cane Cemetery, Abbeville, South Carolina.

Grave of General Samuel McGowan

I'm not a big believer in ghosts, but my buddy Jerry Smith is a strong believer. (He claims he saw one in a clothes basket once. I think it was trying on his dirty underwear.) In 1953, a series of séances were conducted on Fifth Street in New York City. The people conducting the séance were given some pretty accurate details about General McGowan (supposedly by his ghost) and his life after the war when he lived sometime in New York. These people wrote a book called The Fifth Avenue Ghost about these events. The problem I had with the book is the fact that McGowan claimed he was choked to death by the boyfriend of his mistress. Everything I have ever found on the death of McGowan states that he died in South Carolina. Nevertheless, it was interesting and a good read.

From A Diary from Dixie by Mary Boykin Chestnut

One of the great things about working a book like this one is the research. I have gotten to re-read several old favorites over the course of collecting the material for this book. One of these was A Diary from

Dixie, the Civil War Diary of Mary Boykin Chestnut, wife of a US Senator, Confederate General, and member of Columbia, Richmond, and Washington society. It is a great book and gives a vivid picture of the Civil War period with equal attention paid to gossip and hard facts. One of the stories she tells dealing with the antebellum period (though related after the start of the war) deals with the murder of Dr. Thomas Keitt in February 1860 in his sickbed in Columbia County, Florida. Dr. Keitt was a native of what is now Calhoun County and the brother of US Representative Laurence M. Keitt. Congressman Keitt accompanied Preston Brooks to the Senate Chamber when Congressman Brooks caned Senator Charles Sumner for his speech "The Crime Against Kansas." Keitt held off those coming to separate Brooks and Sumner with a pistol and was censured by the House for his actions. He was overwhelmingly re-elected after resigning his seat in protest. Keitt also incited a huge brawl on the floor of the House in 1858 by threatening a Congressman from Pennsylvania. He later served in the Provisional Confederate Congress and as Colonel of both the 20th South Carolina Volunteer Infantry Regiment and later Kershaw's Brigade in the Confederate Army until his death at Cold Harbor in 1864.

Dr. Keitt shared his brother's fire-eating and strongly secessionist politics, but was by all accounts well regarded by the people he enslaved. But the circumstances of his death may belie this. He was advised by a friend that his house servants were poisoning his coffee. Upon the discovery of some white powder in his cup later that day, he threw the dregs into the face of his maid. That night, his throat was cut. Before three slaves were hung, they confessed to slowly dosing him with calomel. Two other slaves were sold. Congressman Keitt declined his share of the estate as being tainted with blood. Dr. Keitt appeared to a family friend a few weeks later and told him that the two men who had escaped hanging were as guilty of his death the others. The appearance occurred when the friend was unaware of Dr. Keitt's murder and was treated as a routine visit until Dr. Keitt vanished before his very eyes. The friend's account was verified by the Congressman when he related the same tale during a visit shortly afterwards. Mrs. Chestnut relates the story as true and I have no reason to doubt her as her diary was not intended for publication at that stage.

The Bonham Family

One oddity about my second book Ghosts of the South Carolina Midlands was that it contained an account of the haunting at the Alamo in San Antonio Texas in the chapter on Saluda County. The reason for this is simple, the commander of the garrison at the Alamo and the last man to seek aid for its defenders were second cousins and natives of the same area of South Carolina. Colonel William Travis commanded the two hundred and fifty men at the Alamo against a force of six thousand trained Mexican troops. Such legends of the West as Jim Bowie and Davy Crockett answered to this son of South Carolina. Colonel Travis sent James Bonham to the garrison at Goliad, seeking reinforcements that never arrived. Bonham returned to the Alamo to die with the other defenders. Travis was killed by a gunshot wound to the head at the site of the first breech of the wall and Bonham was killed manning one of two twelve pound cannons in the chapel and was among the last defenders to die. The Alamo-South Carolina connection is heightened when it is pointed out that James Bonham's younger brother Milledge Luke Bonham served in the United States Army in the Seminole and Mexican Wars and as a general in the Confederate Army (fighting at First Manassas in command of the First Brigade of the Confederate Army of the Potomac). He also served as a Congressman from South Carolina until the secession of his home state in 1860. He served as a Confederate Congressman briefly in 1862 and was elected Governor of South Carolina that same year. At the end of his term, he was appointed a brigadier general in the Confederate Army and served in South Carolina as a recruiter until the end of the war.

The haunting at the Alamo dates from April 1836 after the end of the massacre of the garrison. The Mexican forces retreating from their de-

Governor Milledge Bonham—Brother of Alamo hero, James Bonham, and wartime Governor of South Carolina; Governor Bonham gave Saluda County another tie to the ghosts of the Alamo.

feat at San Jacinto were ordered to tear down the Alamo to honor the high Mexican losses at the hands of the defenders. The chapel, site of the last stand by the defenders was also to be destroyed. Either hands holding torches emerged from the walls deterring the Mexican engineers and their commander, General Andrade or six figures stepped from the walls bearing flaming swords. The six men were reputed to be Colonel Travis, Jim Bowie, Davy Crockett, Isaac Millsaps, John W. Smith, and Captain James Bonham. The booming voice that threatened doom to anyone foolhardy enough to damage the building could have been a practical joker, but the building was left unharmed. During later attempts to change the building, incidents of clanking chains and other odd events led officials to turn the site into a museum. Since the museum opened, cold spots and strange noises have been reported in the long barracks, the site of the fiercest hand to hand combat at the end of the siege. A young man has been seen hiding behind displays in the gift shop, seemingly hiding from pursuers and vanishing when approached, especially as he seems to favor showing up at or near closing time.

General Longstreet at Piedmont Hotel in Gainesville GA (born in Edgefield Co, SC)

The family of Confederate General James Longstreet, who may be better known as Old Pete or Lee's War Horse, has long ties to the State of South Carolina. His uncle, Augustus Longstreet, served as President of the South Carolina College from 1857 to 1860 and is the namesake of the haunted Longstreet Theater on the campus of what is now the University of South Carolina. General Longstreet was born near modern-day North Augusta in Edgefield County, but grew up in Georgia and Alabama. Longstreet entered West Point in 1837 and graduated fifty-fourth out of fifty-six in the class of 1842. One of his best friends during his stay at West Point was Ulysses S. Grant. In fact, Grant married Julia Dent, a fourth cousin of James Longstreet, and James attended the wedding and may have been a groomsman. Longstreet served in the United States Army during the Mexican War and up to the secession of Alabama, when he resigned and returned to Alabama to receive a commission as a Lieutenant Colonel. Upon arriving in Richmond, this commission was superseded by an appointment as a brigadier general in the Confederate Army. His first action in command of his brigade predated First Manassas (First Bull Run) and he would remain in harness until Appomattox. Upon the appointment of Robert E. Lee as commander of the Confederate Army of Northern Virginia, Longstreet became Lee's principal corps commander. Longstreet was an excellent defensive commander, using artillery and terrain to his fullest advantage. However, this reliance on defensive warfare and his post-war career would lead to serious damage to his reputation until recently. He did not perform as well away from Lee, especially during his brief service under Braxton Bragg in the Tennessee theater. Following Grant's appointment as commander of the Union Army of the Potomac, Longstreet recognized that the Confederacy would be hard-pressed for the remainder of the war. Just before Lee met Grant at Appomattox, he told his commander he could expect good and fair terms, but offered to fight on if the terms offered were unsatisfactory. Longstreet joined the Republican Party during Reconstruction, which cost him much of the respect his war record had generated. Longstreet served in several Federal appointive positions, including Ambassador to the Ottoman Empire under President Rutherford B. Hayes. He wrote his memoirs and engaged in controversies defending his war record against his former colleagues in arms until his death in January 1904.

Despite being born in South Carolina, General Longstreet's ghost is encountered in his postwar home of Gainesville, Georgia. The Piedmont Hotel was owned and operated by General Longstreet from 1875 until his death. The General lived at the Piedmont after his house burned in April 1889. The first mention of General Longstreet's return after his death was a mention of sightings of a burly male figure in the steam of arriving locomotives at the Gainesville depot. When the steam cleared, the figure was gone. Reports of the haunting at the Piedmont date to the mid-1990s. A brooding presence, heavy footsteps, odd noises, and the unmistakable aroma of cigar smoke have been reported most often. During renovations, cigarettes and cigarette packs and tools were moved, often from room to room. Footsteps were heard in empty rooms. The sounds of someone exhaling have been heard, often accompanied by the aroma of cigar smoke. One source mentioned a large branch falling from a pecan tree on the grounds in absence of any strong wind or internal weakness and has attributed that event to the General, but I am inclined to doubt that a man as invested in the property as he was would damage it in any way.

Pee Dee Region

McIver-Powe House — Cheraw

After feinting towards Charlotte, North Carolina and Chester, South Carolina, and burning Winnsboro along the way, Sherman and his army veered northeast to head towards Raleigh, North Carolina with the eventual goal of linking up with General Grant's Army of the Potomac in Virginia. His last stop in South Carolina was in Cheraw on the Pee Dee River. During his stay in Cheraw, Sherman used the McIver-Powe home at 143 McIver Street as his sleeping quarters.

According to local lore, a slave girl fumbled the reins of an unidentified Federal officer's mount and he shot her dead on the porch. Unusual noises, being awakened in the night, and noises during phone calls seem to be the hallmarks of this haunting and are blamed on the lady, who may have been a house servant of the McIver family. No mention of the incident is made in any official documents or in Sherman's autobiography. Since Enfield is a private home, I could not gain access to the site to verify the haunting. I would think that additional research is needed to firm up the legendary basis for it though.

Florena Budwin and the Florence National Cemetery

Florena Budwin holds a unique dual claim to fame. She was not only the first female to be buried in a national cemetery, but she was also the first to earn the distinction through her own military service. Hailing from Philadelphia, she enlisted to be near her husband, disguised herself in uniform and took full part in the fighting. This was possible only due to the lack of physical examinations for recruits at the time. The unit that she served in is lost to history, as is the identity of her husband. What is known is that she was captured with her husband in 1864 and sent to the infamous prison camp at Andersonville, Georgia. When that prisoner of war camp closed due to the approach of Sherman's armies en route to Savannah and the sea, the prisoners there were moved to Florence. Florence was chosen because Andersonville was thought to be in Sherman's

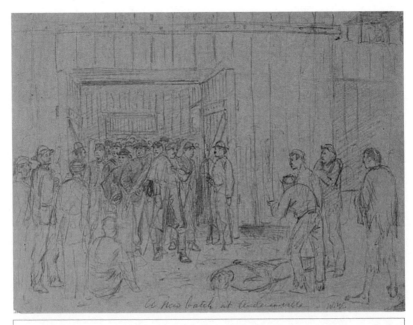

Andersonville Prison, first stop of Florena Budwin and haunted by many of the prisoners who died in harsh conditions.

Florence Stockade, Florence SC — Florena Budwin would have witnessed scenes like this first hand.

line of march following the fall of Atlanta. Between 15,000 and 18,000 prisoners were moved. Limited supplies for both prisoners and guards and overcrowding led to harsh conditions and the death of about 2800 men. The death rate for prisoners at Florence was about twenty-five per day while at Andersonville about one in three prisoners died. Prior to the move, Mr. Budwin was either killed or died of natural causes at Andersonville, though the sources are unclear on the guilty party. In fact the horrid conditions and high death toll at the Prisoner of War camp in Andersonville, better known as Camp Sumter, has left behind several ghost stories and one of the wandering souls seen there even now could well be Florena's husband. Living conditions were so bad at Andersonville, also known as Camp Sumter, that over 13,000 Union prisoners of war died there from 1861 to 1864. There were no buildings at Andersonville, only crude tents that provided little protection from the weather. A swamp ran through the middle of the prison and this contributed greatly to the squalid living conditions in the camp. Scurvy, diarrhea, and dysentery were rampant among the prisoners. There were no latrines or clean drinking water, and little food was supplied to the camp. As bad as conditions were, the Confederacy did have its hands full supporting its own armies and civilians, much less POWs. And the North did not treat its prisoners much better in many cases.

As if the horrible living conditions weren't enough, prisoners also had to fear "the dead line." Any prisoner that crossed the dead line, an imaginary line that marked a boundary between the tents and the stockade wall, was shot immediately by the sentries in the guard towers. Conditions were so inhumane that the Confederate officer that commanded Andersonville, a Swiss-born man named Henry Wirz, was hanged for war crimes after the war ended. In what some would say was a fitting end, the hanging did not break Wirz's neck and thus spectators were treated to the image of his body dancing on the end of the rope until he finally suffocated. The ghost of Captain Henry Wirz can often be seen walking along the roads that lead to Andersonville. However, many say this trial was simple revenge for the horrors of the war and that much of the evidence against Wirz was either exaggerated or fabricated.

People who visit the location of the Andersonville Prison, now preserved as a National Historic Site and National Cemetery, routinely report seeing Union soldiers walking in the woods and fields around the site. When the sun goes down or the weather darkens, especially in the summer, cries of agony can often be heard wafting across the grassy fields and through the rows of tombstones that mark the final resting places of the thousands of former prisoners buried on the site.

Motorists that pass the stockade's cemetery on Georgia Highway 49 state they have seen a Catholic priest standing near a curve in the road on rainy days. This ghost is believed to be Father Peter Whelan. He was a Confederate chaplain who was liked by all—including the prisoners.

Another ghost is seen in Andersonville's cemetery. Multiple witnesses have described this ghost exactly the same way. He has only one leg and is seen hobbling around using a crude crutch. People state that he does not walk on the ground but instead several feet above it.

According to an online account, an unnamed paranormal group had a fairly intense night within the stockade. They heard an individual voice with a pronounced southern drawl demand, "Who goes there?" As the night went on they heard what sounded like a pan being hit with a spoon and a man's voice pleading for "mercy." They heard the sound of a horse galloping across the field in the area where the original prison stood. A fog settled over the field and they saw a campfire and men moving around it. They then smelled the aroma of food cooking. However, back to Florena Budwin…

Shortly after arriving in Florence, Florena's deception was discovered during a routine physical. The ladies of 1864 Florence were astounded and very much put out by the prospect of a widowed female living in the midst of thousands of men and wearing men's clothing at the same time. So they hastily arranged a private room and provided her with suitable clothes. She served as a nurse until her death during an undetermined epidemic in January 1865, a mere month before she would have been released.

Florena Budwin is buried in grave number D-2480, which stands alone even now from her male comrades in arms. Both recent investigations and my own experiences lead me to think that Mrs. Budwin sadly may not rest in peace and that she may not be alone in that respect. I have observed a small ball of greenish-yellow light hovering over her tombstone. Among the trench graves where most of her colleagues lie, both I and other investigators have heard gasps and moans on separate occasions. A moving cold spot has been detected, even in the late fall and early winter. Electromagnetic field (EMF) spikes have also been recorded, which some more scientifically minded ghost researchers think are a sign of the presence of spirits. I am leery of this method of detection, having seen people use these meters without any rudimentary training or any attempts at gaining a base reading.

Mulberry Plantation, near Camden SC — Home of US Senator James Chestnut Junior and his wife and diarist Mary Boykin Chestnut. The house is haunted by a beautiful stallion.

Mulberry Plantation — Kershaw County

The land that is now the site of Mulberry Plantation was granted in 1750 by King George II to the first James Chestnut. The current structure was built in 1820 by the second James Chestnut. The house is best remembered for being the home of the fourth James Chestnut and his wife, Mary Boykin Chestnut, the famed Civil War diarist. The plantation was named a National Historic Landmark in 2000. It is unclear what connection the Chestnut family has with the ghost of Mulberry Plantation. According to local lore, a white stallion dashes through the pines at twilight. I have found only one source for this story, and Mrs. Chestnut does not mention any ghosts at Mulberry in her diary. As mentioned above in the section on the murder of Dr. Thomas Keitt, Mrs. Chestnut was not shy about mentioning the supernatural or uncanny in her diary and did not especially enjoy staying at Mulberry, much preferring Washington, Richmond, or even Columbia. On my two trips past Mulberry, both of which occurred at the appropriate time, I saw no trace of a white horse, living

CIVIL WAR GHOSTS OF SOUTH CAROLINA

or dead. Of course, I could not gain access to all of the more than four thousand acres, as Mulberry is private property.

Rectory Square Park — Camden

According to one source, the sounds of drums beating a call to arms followed by several full-throated "Rebel yells" ring out over Rectory Square Park in downtown Camden. This park is home to a Pantheon dedicated to Camden's six Confederate generals: James Cantey, James Chestnut Junior, Zach Cantey Deas, John Doby Kennedy, Joseph Brevard Kershaw, and John B. Villepigue. The only one not to survive the war was John B. Villepigue, who died of a fever in 1862. Villepigue was also the ancestor of World War I Congressional Medal of Honor winner John C. Villepigue. James Cantey moved to Alabama following his service in the Mexican War and served the Confederacy from that state, but the five others all served from South Carolina. James Chestnut Junior also served as US Senator from South Carolina and was a signer of the Confederate Constitution. Chestnut was the first Senator to resign following the election of President Lincoln. The Pantheon is a pergola, or gazebo, supported by six concrete columns, each of which bears a bronze plaque honoring a general. No apparitions have been seen at the site, but the voices and drums are heard after dark year-round. I have heard neither drums nor yells yet, but I think it is just a matter of being in the right place at the right time.

Woodlawn Plantation — Marion County

Woodlawn Plantation was built in 1853 by the LeGette family. In what I am sure was unintended irony, the house was designed by a free black from Philadelphia and built by slaves. Sadly, none of the records mentions the designer's name. Reverend David LeGette, the builder of Woodlawn, his wife, Martha, and their eldest son, Captain Hannibal LeGette—who, as it happens, died in the house from wounds received in battle in the Civil War—have all been seen at the house by past owners, according to several sources. However, the current owners have an unlisted number and I decided not to breach their privacy with an unannounced visit. I hope you will be as understanding. However, according to Woodlawn's listing on the website, http://south-carolina-plantations.com, as of March 2012, the home and the ten acres of land are for sale for the low price of $220,000. Perhaps you may decide to buy Woodlawn and prove whether or not the LeGettes return or not.

The Church of the Holy Cross — Sumter County

Joel Poinsett, U.S. secretary of war under President Martin Van Buren, is buried at the Episcopal Church of the Holy Cross in Stateburg, South Carolina. Secretary Poinsett also served as a U.S. congressman and as the United States's first minister to Mexico following that country's independence. The church is among the largest rammed-earth construction buildings in the United States and has been a National Historic Landmark since 1973. It is still an active church despite having been built by 1852, so please be respectful during any visits and do not disturb any services or events.

The church cemetery is reputedly the haunt of two apparently unconnected spirits. The first ghost is that of a gentleman dressed in antebellum clothing who strolls between the stones in the cemetery directly behind the church building. I have encountered this ghost briefly. I came around the corner of the building one day while recording some headstone inscriptions and noticed him walking near the brush line at the rear of the property. He paused at my approach and vanished suddenly. Several candidates have been proposed for this unidentified ghost. He may be a Confederate soldier interred in the cemetery; a member of the Frierson family, whose graves were relocated here before the flooding of their burial site in Clarendon County by the waters of Lake Marion in the 1940s; or Secretary Poinsett himself. The figure I saw looked to be in his twenties, so I would venture a guess that the Confederate is the likeliest candidate. Sadly, when my wife Rachel and our friend Erin returned to document sites for this book in the Kershaw and Sumter County areas, we did not receive a return engagement.

Church of the Holy Cross, near Sumter SC — The graveyard of this remarkable church is haunted by several Civil War era specters.

The second ghost is a bit too far-fetched even for me to believe. It involves a woman of unknown age sitting cross-legged in a low-lying tree near the front of the cemetery. No clothing details or any other possible identifying marks have come to my attention. On neither visit did I or the two ladies I was with notice anything out of the ordinary, despite our best efforts.

Oakland Plantation — Sumter County

Oakland Plantation near Hagood was the seat of the Sanders family from 1735 to 1981. The first structure on the site was a public house or tavern. The current house dates from 1816 and was built by Williams Sanders IV. In fact, modern Hagood was originally named Sanders Junction, only changing its name with the election of Johnson Hagood as governor in the 1880s. According to local accounts, the house still stands due to the beauty of the daughter of William Sanders V, Georgia, whose charms so struck Major General Potter that he returned to Hagood after the war to woo her. Sadly, he would be disappointed, as she had already married a local. Given his role in devastating the Pee Dee and Sandhills area, I doubt his suit would have carried much weight, considering that the house was known as Dixie Hall from the 1950s. Even considering its use as a headquarters for both Major Generals Potter and P.M.B. Young and as a field hospital, the house was still struck by a stray artillery shell. However, the haunting surprisingly has nothing to do with its use as a field hospital. The ghost is supposed to be William Sanders IV, grandfather of Georgia Sanders, who cut his throat after his favorite daughter married a man that he disapproved of. He is supposed to have repented with his last breath and still paces about. He is reputed to be the house's protector. Sadly, I cannot verify Mr. Sanders's continued presence, as I could not arrange an invitation to Oakland and did not wish to intrude.

Battle of Dinkins Mill — Sumter County

The Battle of Dinkins Mill was part of the larger campaign connected with Potter's Raid on the Pee Dee region of South Carolina to destroy whatever railroad stock and military supplies could be found. The roots of Potter's Raid are found in Sherman's march out of South Carolina on his way to North Carolina. As Sherman's forces departed Columbia, South Carolina, he ordered his troops to take a line of March to the northeast. His intention was to convince the confederate command that he was headed to Charlotte, North Carolina, while his real intention was to move toward eastern North Carolina. A cavalry raid was directed towards Charlotte, which caught the attention of most Confederate troops in the state. With confederate troops out of his path he ordered the federal troops to move east through Cheraw and toward Bentonville and Raleigh. Sherman's maneuvers meant that the area around Kershaw and Sumter Counties remained untouched by Sherman's main force. Large numbers of railroad locomotives and rolling stock were moved to that area on the lines of the South Carolina R.R. and the Wilmington and

Manchester R.R. In addition, large amounts of military stores had also been stockpiled in the same region as Sherman's troops approached Columbia. Sherman learned of the trapped stores and railroad equipment and ordered that they be destroyed. Major General Q.A. Gillmore ordered a provisional division assembled under the command of Brigadier General Edward E. Potter. Potter was ordered to destroy the railroads in the area between Florence, Sumter, and Camden. Potter took command of the provisional division on 1 April, 1865 at Georgetown. The division numbered 2,700 men, including the famous 54th Massachusetts and two other regiments of US Colored Troops. Porter marched out of Georgetown on 5 April, 1865.

On Easter Day, April 9, 1865, the Battle of Dingle's Mill was fought three miles south of present-day Sumter, then called Sumterville. Early in the morning, General Edward E. Potter's army, called Potter's Raiders, came from the direction of Kingstree. This put them north of the pond at Dingle's Mill and across Turkey Creek. Confederate militiamen dug in their heels behind makeshift breastworks and awaited the arrival of the Union forces. The two working pieces of Confederate artillery were commanded by Lt. William Alexander McQueen and Lt. Pamerya, an artilleryman from New Orleans who was in the hospital at Sumter. A third piece of artillery was too rusted to work. General Potter ordered an attack from the left and rear. The 54th was a part of this flanking column. Unable to reach the Rebels's position, the United States Colored Troops countermarched to where Colonel Brown's First Brigade was stationed on the main road. Hallowell's brigade rejoined the main force later in the afternoon. Lt. McQueen was incapacitated and Lt. Pamerya was killed. The Confederate forces fell back toward Sumterville in the face of overwhelming odds after these losses. They made one more stand, but left the field of battle about six in the evening, ending the battle. At about this same time, General Robert E. Lee was meeting with General Ulysses S. Grant at Appomattox Courthouse, three hundred miles away. Southern losses were six killed, seven wounded, two captured. Northern losses were four killed, twenty-three wounded. Later that day, Federal troops under Gen. Edward E. Potter occupied Sumter. They destroyed railroad property, burned cotton and the jail, ransacked businesses, and looted homes. Potter, whose headquarters was at the present courthouse site on Main Street, left Sumter on April 11. At Boykins Mill, on April 18, in one of the last engagements of the war, a small force of Confederate regulars and local Home Guard fought a defensive action against Potter's Raiders which delayed their advance for a day.

Following the battle of Boykin's Mill, Federal troops commanded by Brig. Gen. Edward E. Potter advanced south to just below the town of Stateburg. Here, at Dinkins Mill, on April 19, they attacked and attempted to flank a Confederate force commanded by Maj. Gen. P.M.B. Young, which defended this crossing. After slight losses on both sides, most of the Confederate force withdrew towards Beech Creek.

During a road trip to gather material and visit sites for my book Ghosts of the Pee Dee a few summers ago, my wife Rachel and I and our friend Erin Maloney took a drive down SC Highways 97 and 261 and US Highway 521 to visit sites in Camden, Kershaw County, Sumter, Stateburg, and Sumter County. After a successful trip and much fun (but no ghostly encounters), we were headed home about six in the afternoon north on Highway 261 when my wife asked if anyone else had seen that man standing in the ruins of the old mill. Erin and I both said no and I turned around as soon as I could. When we returned to the site, I stopped at the historic marker commemorating the skirmish and asked where she had seen the man and what he looked like. She described a solid-looking man in gray standing at the corner of the second floor looking out at the road. However, the spot she pointed out was missing any flooring or cross beams and the underbrush had not been disturbed in some time, much less in the past few minutes. There was no sign of any one but us with sight either on Dinkins Mill Road or on the highway itself. My wife shrugged it off and we continued home. I have ridden past that spot several times since and have never seen anything, but my eyes do seem drawn to it, regardless of the time of day or season of the year when I pass.

Loch Dhu Plantation

Loch Dhu Plantation is located in Berkeley County and was the home of the Kirk family for almost one hundred fifty years. Part of the grounds are now under the waters of Lake Marion. The name is Gaelic for "black lake." One of the outbuildings was relocated from General Francis Marion's plantation Pond Bluff (now submerged under Lake Marion). The home is privately owned, so please do not trespass. The haunting at Loch Dhu seems to be connected the home's service as a hospital during the Civil War. The owner, Dr. Philip S. Kirk was a Confederate surgeon and his daughters served as his nurses. When Union troops arrived to burn Loch Dhu, the Kirks and their patients refused to leave, sparing the house. Local legend claims that heavy boot steps are heard pacing the upstairs hallway and on the staircase. As well, the interior doors open and close unaided by living hands. The footsteps are either those of Dr. Kirk checking on patients or those of the Union soldiers attempting to persuade the Kirks to leave their home to the torch. Since no reported apparitions have been seen, we may never know.

Coastal Region

General Beauregard Prowls Charleston's City Hall and Refights a Losing Battle at His Former Home

Pierre Gustave Toutant Beauregard was a Louisiana-born American military officer, politician, inventor, writer, civil servant, and the first prominent general of the Confederate States Army during the American Civil War. Beauregard was trained as a civil engineer at the United States Military Academy and served with distinction as an engineer in the Mexican-American War. Following a brief appointment as Superintendent of West Point in 1861, and upon the South's secession, he became the first Confederate brigadier general. He commanded the defenses of Charleston, South Carolina, at the start of the Civil War at Fort Sumter on April 12, 1861. Three months later, he was the victor at the First Battle of Bull Run near Manassas, Virginia. Beauregard commanded armies in the Western Theater, including at the Battle of Shiloh in Tennessee, and the Siege of Corinth in northern Mississippi. He returned to Charleston and defended it from repeated naval and land attacks in 1863. He later

Charleston City Hall — Does General Beauregard still stalk the halls looking out for corruption?

served in Petersburg in 1864.

In April 1865, Beauregard and General Joseph E. Johnston convinced Davis and the remaining cabinet members that the war needed to end. Johnston surrendered most of the remaining armies of the Confederacy, including Beauregard and his men, to Maj. Gen. William T. Sherman. Beauregard pursued a position in the Brazilian Army in 1865, but declined the Brazilians's offer and also declined offers to take command of the armies of Romania and Egypt. Beauregard passed away in 1893 and is buried in Metairie Cemetery in New Orleans.

The City Hall in Charleston began its life as a branch of the First Bank of the United States in 1801. In 1818, the building became City Hall and has survived fires, earthquakes, bombardments, and several tropical storms and hurricanes. As noted above, Beauregard served as the commanding General in the Charleston theater twice and enjoyed most of his successes there. In honor of his defense of the city, two different portraits of the General hang in the building. The ghost of General Beauregard has been seen wandering the halls of the building. No solid reason for his return appeared during my research, but speculation is that either his ego has called him back to the scene of one of his greatest triumphs or that he returns when the city is in jeopardy of some kind. His first appearance has been linked to an incident of embezzlement by a city employee just after the start of the Civil War, but the General spared the good name of the embezzler. The other haunting connected to General Beauregard is located at his former home in New Orleans, Louisiana— the Beauregard-Keyes House. The haunting is claimed to occur at two very different times. One version claims the events occur nightly and the other claims that the haunting only happens on the anniversary of the events in question. Due to the nature of the haunting, I am inclined to believe the anniversary theory myself.

First, some background is needed on the Battle of Shiloh. The Battle of Shiloh, also known as the Battle of Pittsburg Landing, was a major battle in the Western Theater of the American Civil War, fought April 6–7, 1862, in southwestern Tennessee. A Union army under Maj. Gen. Ulysses S. Grant had moved via the Tennessee River deep into Tennessee and was encamped principally at Pittsburg Landing on the west bank of the river. Confederate forces under Generals Albert Sidney Johnston and P. G. T. Beauregard launched a surprise attack on Grant there. The Confederates achieved considerable success on the first day, but were ultimately defeated on the second day. On the first day of the battle, the Confederates struck with the intention of driving the Union defenders away from the river and into the swamps of Owl Creek to the west, hoping to defeat Grant's Army of the Tennessee before the anticipated arrival of Maj. Gen. Don Carlos Buell's Army of the Ohio. The Confederate battle lines became confused during the fierce fighting, and Grant's men instead fell back to the northeast, in the direction of Pittsburg Landing. A position on a slightly sunken road, nicknamed the "Hornet's Nest,", defended by the men of Brig. Gens. Benjamin M. Prentiss's and W. H. L. Wallace's divisions provided critical time for the rest of the Union line to stabilize under the protection of numerous artillery batteries. Gen. Johnston was killed during the first day of fighting, and Beauregard, his second in command, decided against assaulting the final Union position that night. Reinforcements from Gen. Buell and from Grant's own army arrived in the evening and turned the tide the next morning, when the Union commanders launched a counterattack along the entire line. The Confederates were forced to retreat from the bloodiest battle in United States history up to that time, ending their hopes that they could block the Union advance into northern Mississippi. The two-day battle of Shiloh, the costliest in American history up to that time, resulted in the defeat of the Confederate army and frustration of Johnston's plans to prevent the joining of the two Union armies in Tennessee. Union casualties were 13,047 (1,754 killed, 8,408 wounded, and 2,885 missing); Grant's army bore the brunt of the fighting over the two days, with casualties of 1,513 killed, 6,601 wounded, and 2,830 missing or captured. Confederate casualties were 10,699 (1,728 killed, 8,012 wounded, and 959 missing or captured). The dead included the Confederate army's commander, Albert Sidney Johnston. According to legend, on the night of April 6, the drawing room of the Beauregard-Keyes Mansion is converted into the site of the Battle of Shiloh. The entire Confederate army appears in full dress uniform on the staircase with Generals Johnston and Beauregard at its head. Over the course of the night, the soldiers are reduced to the condition they were in at the end of the battle, wearing torn and bloody uniforms, while gore and gun smoke permeates the room. Just before dawn, General Beauregard appears at the foot of the staircase and leads his beaten men up them; the men vanish as they mount the stairs.

Now, I sincerely doubt that anyone could stand living with this on a nightly basis, so I tend to agree with the anniversary-only theory. But, as I have not yet had a chance to visit the Beauregard-Keyes Mansion, I will have to remain in suspense. Stories are also told of a voice being heard coming from the Mansion after the death of the General hoarsely gasping "Shiloh" over and over. The General has been seen staring from the windows facing Chartres Street and dancing with a woman thought to be his second wife in the ballroom as well.

Battery Carriage House Inn

The Battery Carriage House Inn at 20 South Battery is one of Charleston's best know bed and breakfasts. During the Civil War it was located on an active military post and was abandoned and was slightly damaged as were many of the houses on the Battery. One of the best known ghosts at the Inn is known as the Headless Torso. This entity is mainly

Battery Carriage House Inn in Charleston is home to several ghosts with Civil War connections.

found in Room Eight and is described as a barrel-chested man without any limbs or head. Witnesses reported feelings of dread, terror, and impending harm when the spirit is present. This spirit is thought to be either a victim of the bombardment of Charleston in 1863 by the Union forces that surrounded the city or of one of the many fires to have swept the city in the 19th Century. Another ghost known to haunt Room Eight is known as the Gentleman Ghost. He appears to single ladies as a wispy apparition who lies down on the bed next to them. When they scream he gets up and disappears through the nearest wall. He is thought to be the college-age son of some previous owner who jumped to his death early in the 20th Century. However, one source mentioned that the headless torso appeared to a workman on the roof in the 1930s. The shock caused the worker to fall to his death. The workman has also been seen on the grounds as well. The shutters on the windows and opened and closed by themselves in several rooms and a strange glow has been reported in Room Three.

Folly Island and Morris Island

Cool but Creepy Folly Island is a Sea Island located to the south of Charleston that is known as "the Edge of America" and is one of the better spots to surf on the Atlantic coast of the United States. During the late 1600s and early 1700s, Folly and Morris Islands were heavily used by pirates as hiding places. Folly Island is currently inhabited, though Morris Island is now deserted and under serious threat from erosion and only exists at low tide. Folly Island fell to Union troops in April 1863 although a small skirmish in May of that year was the only actual fighting on the island. Folly Island was used as a staging area for the two assaults on the Confederate stronghold of Fort Wagner in July 1863. The Confederates abandoned the post in September 1863 after the fresh water on the base became unsafe. The sightings of Civil War soldiers in full uniform may be related to mass graves found on the island in 1999 containing those killed during the two assaults on Fort Wagner. The first

Morris Island, near Charleston SC — The site of the attack on Fort Wagner by the 54th Massachusetts Colored Infantry, Morris Island is the site of several hauntings.

assault on the Fort occurred on July 10; Union artillery on Folly Island (which had been occupied in April 1863) and naval gunfire from Rear Admiral John A. Dahlgren's four ironclad warships bombarded the Confederate defenses protecting the southern end of Morris Island. This provided cover for the landing of Brig. Gen. George C. Strong's brigade, which crossed Lighthouse Inlet and landed at the southern tip of the island. Strong's troops advanced, capturing several batteries, moving about three miles to within range of Fort Wagner. Also known as Battery Wagner, it was a heavily gunned redoubt that covered nearly the entire width of the northern end of Morris Island, facing Sumter. The Union columns captured the outlying batteries and the crest of the ridge. On July 11, Strong's brigade attacked at dawn, advancing through a thick fog, attempting to seize Fort Wagner. Although the men of the 7th Connecticut Infantry overran a line of rifle pits, they were repulsed by the 1,770-

man force under Confederate Col. Robert F. Graham. Heavy artillery fire from Fort Wagner prevented other units from joining the attack. Union casualties were 339 (49 killed, 123 wounded, 167 missing), Confederate casualties were twelve.

The second Battle of Fort Wagner is far better known, largely due to the 1989 film Glory that starred Matthew Broderick, Denzel Washington, Cary Elwes, and Morgan Freeman depicting the raising and training of the 54th Massachusetts Volunteer Infantry that climaxed with a depiction of the unsuccessful assault by the 54th. Fort Wagner was commanded by Brigadier General William B. Taliaferro and Brigadier General (and later Governor of South Carolina) Johnson Hagood. Gillmore also ordered an artillery bombardment of the fort. The fort was on a very narrow island so the Union forces could only assault the fort with one regiment at a time. The approach to the fort was constricted to a strip of beach sixty yards wide with the ocean to the east and the marsh from Vincent's Creek to the west. Upon rounding this defile, the Union Army was presented with the 250-yard south face of Fort Wagner, which stretched from Vincent's creek to the sea. Surrounding the fort was a shallow moat riveted with sharpened palmetto logs and an abatis, while the moat on the seaward side had spike-bearing planks positioned beneath the water. Gilmore ordered his siege guns and mortars to begin a bombardment of fort on July 18 and they were joined by the naval gunfire from six monitors that pulled to within 300 yards of the fort. The bombardment lasted eight hours, but caused little damage against the sandy walls of the fort, and in all, killed only about eight men and wounded an additional twenty, as the defenders had taken cover in the bombproof shelter. The 54th Massachusetts, an infantry regiment composed of African-American soldiers led by Colonel Robert Gould Shaw, led the Union attack at dusk. Shaw was killed upon the parapet early in the action. Some confederate reports claim his body was pierced seven times, with the fatal wound a rifle bullet to his chest. In all, 1,515 Union soldiers were killed, captured, or wounded in the assault of July 18. Only 315 men were left from the

54th after the battle. William Carney, an African-American sergeant with the 54th, is considered the first black recipient of the Medal of Honor for his actions that day in recovering and returning the unit's U.S. Flag to Union lines. Confederate casualties numbered 174.

The afore-mentioned sightings of Civil War soldiers on full uniform on Folly Island are centered on the now uninhabited area of the island that face the famous Morris Island Light. The remains of Morris Island are marked solely by the Light as the island is only visible at low tide; however, tourists have reported seeing a woman in a white dress with a white apron in the doorway of the lighthouse. The lighthouse is only accessible by boat and entry is not permitted. Some people have even reported seeing the former keeper's house in front of the Light, though it was destroyed by Hurricane Hugo in 1989. I have seen a figure in Confederate gray standing on the beach at the end of the trail leading to the Light. Others have seen him walking towards the Light, completely oblivious to the water that should be up to his chest. My wife and I have walked to the end of Folly Island nearest the Light several times. Though she has not seen anything unusual, she has often commented on the sense of being watched and that someone was waiting for us to leave. The former roadway leading to the Light is now closed and is lined by concrete slabs marking home sites destroyed by Hurricane Hugo's passing. It is a bit disquieting to be there at dusk or twilight to say the least.

Forts Moultrie and Sumter

South Carolina patriots began to build a fort to guard Charleston, South Carolina, harbor in 1776. British Admiral Sir Peter Parker with nine British warships attacked the fort—still unnamed and incomplete—on June 28, 1776, near the beginning of the American Revolutionary War. The soft palmetto logs did not crack under bombardment but rather absorbed the shot; cannon balls reportedly even bounced off the walls of the structure. William Moultrie commanded the 2nd South Carolina Regiment for the revolutionary patriots in this battle. The fort took its

Fort Moultrie — Best known as a Revolutionary War site, this fort played a role in the conflict over Fort Sumter.

name Fort Moultrie in his honor. The British eventually captured Fort Moultrie in the Siege of Charleston in spring 1780. Nevertheless, the colonists won the war, and British troops departed in 1782, at which time the flag was presented in Charleston, by General Greene, commander of the southern Regulars.

Great Britain and France began another war in 1793, heightening tensions. The United States of America thence embarked on a systematic fortification of important harbors. Atop the decayed original Fort Moultrie, the Army completed a new fort in 1798; the Army also built nineteen other new forts along the Atlantic coast. A hurricane destroyed Fort Moultrie in 1804, and a brick fort replaced it in 1809. Fort Moultrie changed little over the next five decades. The Army altered the parapet and modernized the

armament, but defense of Charleston centered increasingly around newly
created Fort Sumter. By the time of the American Civil War, Fort Moultrie,
Fort Sumter, Fort Johnson, and Castle Pinckney surrounded and defended
Charleston. Fort Moultrie nevertheless began to record meteorological ob-
servations in the early 1820s. The Army detained Seminole Indian fighter
Osceola and some fellow Seminole prisoners at Fort Moultrie in late 1837.
Osceola died of malaria in January 1838; the Army buried his corpse at
Fort Moultrie and thereafter maintained his grave. Edgar Allan Poe served
at the Fort in the late 1820s, under an alias, writing his story The Gold-Bug
there. William T. Sherman served at Fort Moultrie in the 1840s as a Lieutenant. His return to South Carolina in 1865 would not prove to be happy
homecoming. South Carolina seceded from the Union on December 20,
1860. Unlike their counterparts at the other forts, defenders of Fort Moultrie chose not to surrender to the South Carolina forces. On December 26,
1860, Union Major Robert Anderson moved his garrison at Fort Moultrie
to the stronger Fort Sumter. On February 8, 1861, South Carolina joined
other seceded Deep Southern states to form the Confederate States of
America. In April 1861, Confederate troops shelled Fort Sumter into sub-
mission and the American Civil War began. In April 1863, Federal iron-
clads and shore batteries began a bombardment of Fort Moultrie and the
other forts around Charleston harbor. Over the ensuing twenty months,
Union bombardment reduced Fort Sumter to a rubble pile and pounded
Fort Moultrie below a sand hill, which protected it against further Union
bombardment. The rifled cannon proved its superiority to brickwork fortifications but not to the endurance of the Confederate artillerymen, who
continued to man Fort Moultrie. In February 1865, the Confederate Army
finally abandoned the rubble of Fort Moultrie and evacuated the city of
Charleston, South Carolina. The Army modernized Fort Moultrie in the
1870s with huge rifled cannon and deep concrete bunkers. Seacoast defense of the United States ceased as a viable strategy by 1947.

No ghost stories from Fort Moultrie date from the Civil War, but earlier ones do exist. The best known of these tales concerns the famed

Seminole Indian chief Osceola who was imprisoned here for about four months until his death in 1838. According to legend, Osceola's spirit totem was a pelican. After his capture under a flag of truce, a pelican is supposed to have dove at his captors's heads repeatedly. After his arrival at Moultrie, Osceola reputedly cursed Charleston, which is supposed to have been fulfilled by the earthquake of 1886, in the decades since his death. Just prior to major events in the history of the city, witnesses have reported seeing a white pelican near the cell that housed Osceola. If approached, the bird vanishes.

Named after General Thomas Sumter, Revolutionary War hero, Fort Sumter was built following the War of 1812, as one of a series of fortifications on the southern U.S. coast. Construction began in 1829, and the structure was still unfinished in 1861, when the Civil War began. The fort was a five-sided brick structure, 170 to 190 feet long, with walls five feet thick, standing 50 feet over the low tide mark. It was designed to house 650 men and 135 guns in three tiers of gun emplacements, although it was never filled near its full capacity. However, the most famous period of activity at the Fort was to begin shortly. On December 26, 1860, six days after South Carolina declared its secession, U.S. Army Major Robert Anderson abandoned the indefensible Fort Moultrie and secretly relocated companies E and H (127 men, 13 of them musicians) of the 1st U.S. Artillery to Fort Sumter on his own initiative, without orders from Washington. He thought that providing a stronger defense would delay an attack by South Carolina militia. Over the next few months repeated calls for evacuation of Fort Sumter from the government of South Carolina and then from Confederate Brigadier General P. G. T. Beauregard were ignored. Union attempts to resupply and reinforce the garrison were repulsed on January 9, 1861 when the first shots of the war, fired by cadets from The Citadel, prevented the steamer Star of the West, hired to transport troops and supplies to Fort Sumter, from completing the task. After realizing that Anderson's command would run out of food by April 15, 1861, President Lincoln ordered a fleet of ships, under the command of Gustavus V. Fox, to attempt entry into Charleston Harbor and support Fort Sumter. On Thursday, April 11, 1861, Beauregard sent three aides, Colonel James Chesnut, Jr., Captain Stephen D. Lee, and Lieutenant A. R. Chisolm to demand the surrender of the fort. Anderson declined, and the aides returned to report to Beauregard. The aides then left the fort and proceeded to the nearby Fort Johnson. There, Chesnut ordered the fort to open fire on Fort Sumter. On Friday, April 12, 1861, at 4:30 AM, Confederate batteries opened fire, firing for thirty-four straight hours on the fort. Edmund Ruffin, noted Virginian agronomist and secessionist, claimed that he fired the first shot on Fort Sumter. His story has been widely believed, but others have also claimed the honor. No attempt was made to return the fire for more than two hours. The fort's supply of ammunition was not suited for the task, also there were no fuses for their explosive shells, only solid balls could be used against the Rebel batteries. At about 7:00 AM, Captain Abner Doubleday, the fort's second in command, was given the honor of firing the first shot in defense of the fort. On Saturday, April 13, the fort was surrendered and evacuated. During the attack, the Union colors fell. Lt. Norman J. Hall risked life and limb to put them back up. No Union soldiers died in the actual battle though a Confederate soldier bled to death having been wounded by a misfiring cannon. One Union soldier died and another was mortally wounded during the forty-seventh shot of a one hundred-shot salute, allowed by the Confederacy. Afterwards the salute was shortened to fifty shots. The Star of the West took all the Union soldiers to New York City. The Fort came under serious fire again on April 7, 1863, when Rear Admiral Samuel Francis Du Pont, commander of the South Atlantic Blockading Squadron and co-leader of the successful Union assault on Port Royal, South Carolina, led an attack against the harbor's defenses. The attack was unsuccessful. After the devastating bombardment, both General Quincy A. Gillmore and Rear Admiral John A. Dahlgren were determined to launch a boat assault on Fort Sumter for the night of September 8–9, 1863. The Union sailors and marines who did land could not scale the wall. The Confederates fired upon the landing party and as well as throwing hand grenades and masonry. The boats that could withdraw did so, and

Fort Sumter at the end of the War—Four years of Union attacks and bombardment took a heavy toll on Sumter.

the landing party surrendered. The Union casualties were eight killed, nineteen wounded, and 105 captured (including fifteen of the wounded). The Confederates did not suffer any casualties in the assault. After the unsuccessful boat assault, the bombardment recommenced and proceeded with varying degree of intensity, doing more damage to Fort Sumter until the end of the war. The garrison continued to suffer casualties. The Confederates continued to salvage guns and other material from the ruins. The last Confederate Commander, Major Thomas A. Huguenin, never surrendered Fort Sumter, but General William T. Sherman's advance through South Carolina finally forced the Confederates to evacuate Charleston on February 17, 1865 and abandon Fort Sumter. The Federal government formally took possession of Fort Sumter on February 22, 1865 with a flag raising ceremony. Fifty-two Confederate soldiers were killed there during the remainder of the war. While a number of slaves were killed while working at the fort, the exact number is unknown. When the Civil War ended, Fort Sumter was in ruins.

The haunting at Fort Sumter is directly related to the death that occurred during the one-hundred gun salute at the surrender ceremony. The only casualty, Private Daniel Hough, was killed when the gun he was manning misfired and exploded. Blemishes on the last Union flag to fly over the Fort before it fell (known as the Storm Flag and on display at the Fort museum) and on the first Confederate flag to fly over it (the Palmetto Guards flag) are supposed to be the face or profile of Private Hough. I think people are imposing a familiar pattern on a stain, but others see it more clearly. Other reports of odd activity fall into a bit more "normal" range such as voices from empty rooms, the stink of gunpowder, and reports of an apparition of a bearded man in blue. I have seen the man in blue, but did not know that the Fort was supposedly haunted. I was visiting the Fort with my fourth-grade class back in the early 1980s, when something caught my eye during the tour. I saw a figure in a blue jacket and pants walk into a casemate, or fortified gun emplacement and not come out. When I questioned the ranger about the man, he told me that no one was wearing that uniform on the site and that area was closed to visitors. As our visit happened in the spring, I wonder if I saw Private Hough reporting for duty. I have not seen anything else on subsequent visits however.

Mount Pleasant

Due to the central role played by Charleston in the decades before secession and after, it is only natural that the surrounding communities should have ghost lore from the era themselves. One such place is Mount Pleasant, located just cross the Cooper River (and the Arthur Ravenel Bridge) from Charleston. Patriots Point, now home of the aircraft carrier USS Yorktown and other historic ships is one of the main launching points for the ferry to Fort Sumter. One notable fact about Mount Pleasant is that it was the site of one of the first public meetings to pass secession resolutions if Abraham Lincoln were elected President, which even pre-dated Lincoln's election. On September 24, 1860, a public meeting was held in Mount Pleasant. Eleven total resolutions were introduced and passed. The 10th and 11th resolutions were determinations to leave the United States should Abraham Lincoln be elected president: "Resolved that in the opinion of this meeting, the election of Mr. Lincoln to the office of President of the United States is in itself sufficient cause for war;" and "Resolved that in the event of Mr. Lincoln's election South Carolina should make every effort to meet one or more of the other southern states in convention to determine the best mode of dissolving the connection with the present union." In December, the Secession Convention gathered in Charleston and took the advice offered by the folks at Mount Pleasant, among others.

There are three ghost legends dating from the Civil War concerning Mount Pleasant. Sadly, I have not been able to find more than one source for each, and I have not personally experienced any of them yet. The first concerns a church known as the Easter Sunday Church. This church was going to be targeted for "destruction." With people attending inside, the Yankees surrounded the church and opened fire without warning, murdering all those in attendance. Years and decades later some of the locals would attempt to paint or wallpaper over the blood stains on the walls. In less than twenty-four hours, the blood would seep through and remain fresh to the touch. Despite my best efforts and the assistance of a family friend, Amy Ravenel, who then worked at the Mount Pleasant branch of the Charleston County Library, I can find no record of any such massacre in Mount Pleasant or anywhere else in South Carolina. The likeliest suspect for the church in question in my opinion is the Mount Pleasant Presbyterian Church. It was erected about 1854 and originally a Congregational Church affiliated with Old Wappetaw Church, founded about 1699. The building served as a Confederate hospital during the Civil War, then briefly housed the Laing School for Freedmen during Reconstruction. This service might explain the bloodstains, if any are present. The church was rededicated and renamed Mount Pleasant Presbyterian Church in 1870.

Another legend concerning Mount Pleasant is the story of the Army of the Dead. Supposedly, every night at midnight the sounds of heavy wheels and marching feet ring out. The legend states that no one witnessed the procession until a laundress disobeyed her husband and watched one night. She saw and heard the passing of an army, complete with cavalry troops, marching infantry, cannon, wagons, and ambulances. Upon the sound of a distant bugle the procession faded leaving no trace of its passage. The men wore gray and were supposedly soldiers who had died in the hospitals in Charleston without hearing about Lee's surrender and were attempting to reinforce that beleaguered General in Virginia. After watching the procession, the laundress was afflicted with a paralyzed arm that she blamed on her disobedience and intrusion. I have not yet had the pleasure of encountering the Army of the Dead, but I have hopes of seeing them one of these days.

The final legend concerning Mount Pleasant is closely related to the Army of the Dead, but is more closely connected to the tragic tale of the crew of the Confederate submarine, the *CSS Hunley*. They are known as the Night Rangers and their indistinct voices and footsteps have been heard near Breach Inlet on the Cooper River for over a century, but no one has ever seen them. About 5:00 AM or earlier seems to be the best time to hear the Night Rangers pass long the old waterfront of Mount Pleasant. Not being a morning person, I have not yet experienced this and doubt I will anytime soon, but witnesses report encountering them as recently as 2004. The *CSS Hunley* was launched for the final time from Breach Inlet on February 17, 1864. Two other launches had ended in failure and death for the crews, including the *Hunley*'s builder Horace Hunley. The eight men knew that they might not return, but keeping Charleston Harbor open for blockade runners was vital. The target was the *USS Housatonic*. The crew of the *Housatonic* opened fire on the *Hunley* with small arms, to no effect. The *Hunley* rammed a spar torpedo into the hull of the *Housatonic*, which sank with lost of five crew members out of a total of 160. The *Hunley* sank a short distance away with the loss of the entire crew. The *Hunley* was recovered in 2000 and the wreck of the *Housatonic* was scrapped by 1890.

Sentry on the Bohicket

The following story was told to me by a dear family friend, Susan Roddey, who is a native of Johns Island. On the side of the Bohicket River next to Rockville Presbyterian Church there sits a concrete bench. While Susan was in high school, some of her friends and she decided to hang out on the riverbank, just before dark. After about ten minutes, one of the girls present saw a male figure approaching. As he came closer, she noticed his thick mustache and bloody face. She screamed and everyone scattered back to their cars. Susan has since determined that the man

Rockville Presbyterian Church, near Charleston SC- Does a long dead sentry still keep watch over the Bohicket?

must have been a sentry who was murdered on duty as she saw him turn and return back the way he came just after passing by the concrete bench as they backed out. Given the site's relative proximity to Bloody Dick Swamp, where a similar figure has been seen, it is possible that the two ghosts could be one and the same. Despite several trips to Johns Island and Rockville, I have not encountered either gentleman yet, but I'm sure it will just be a matter of time.

Sword Gate or Mme. Talvande Still Watches Over Her Girls

The story of the haunting at 32 Legare Street in Charleston is one of the better-known bits of ghost lore from that holiest of Holy Cities (where the Ashley and Cooper Rivers join to form the Atlantic Ocean according to local wits). I had not thought to include it in this book until I read in her diary that Mary Boykin Chestnut attended Mme. Talvande's French School for Young Ladies from 1835 to 1839. Given Mrs. Chestnut's pivotal role in chronicling so many events during the Civil War period, I felt it was a natural fit for this book. Another tie to the Civil War era is that Jessie Lincoln Randolph, a granddaughter of President Lincoln owned the house in the 1930s, but never lived there. First some history is required. The house at 32 Legare Street was built in 1803 and was acquired by Andre' (or Andrew) Talvande and his wife Ann who moved to Charleston from Sainte-Domingue, which is now known as Haiti following its revolution in 1803. They were just two of many refugees to flee to Charleston over the next few years. The Talvandes were welcomed by Charleston society and quickly entrusted with the care and social education of their daughters. Things went very well until the late 1820s when a young lady named Maria Whaley arrived from her family's plantation on Edisto Island. Miss Whaley was enrolled at Mme. Talvande's to distract her from a suitor, a young New Yorker named George Morris. Morris was unacceptable to Mr. Whaley for several reasons. First, he was neither from Charleston nor from its "better half." Secondly, Maria's reaction to the mere presence of George Morris concerned Mr. Whaley. He knew she would soon accept no one suitor, even one of her father's choosing. Despite the busy social and educational duties at Mme. Talvande's, George and Maria met again and began to plan a life together, regardless of parental opposition. On March 8, 1829, Maria scaled the wall and dashed to Saint Michael's Church, where she and George were married. She returned to school and, thanking her luck, awaited George's arrival the next morning. Mr. Morris came to collect his bride the next day asking for Mrs. Morris. Despite being told that Mme. Talvande was the only married woman present, he persisted and Maria stepped forward as his bride. Despite initial opposition to the match, Mr. Whaley was eventually reconciled to the marriage. The story continues that Mme. Talvande was humiliated by the elopement and felt that she was forever guilty in the eyes of the parents of her other charges, even though the school stayed open until 1848 and thrived. The rumor that a high brick wall, topped with broken bottles, on the property dates from just after the elopement is false as the wall dates from before 1819 when the Talvandes bought the property. Reports of the apparition of a woman walking the halls and entering the bedrooms, the front door opening, and heavy footsteps being heard in the house, and the spirit of a young man in either Cavalier or antebellum dress in the dining room began after the Civil War and continue to circulate. The Sword Gates at the front of the house were made in the late 1830s for the Guard House, but the extra pair of gates were purchased by a later owner and installed at the house. As of the spring of 2012, the Sword gate House was for sale for the price of just twenty-three million dollars, so you may be able to buy it and prove whether or not Mme. Talvande still checks on her girls or not.

Trapman Street Tales

The following stories are abstracted from the wonderful book "Doctor to the Dead" by John Bennett, one of the better older sources on haunts and legends in Charleston. Trapman Street in Charleston is now a quiet residential street just north of Broad Street in downtown. But during the

Civil War and after the battle of Secessionville, it was home to one of the busiest military hospitals in Charleston. The hospital stood at the corner of Trumbo Court and Trapman Street and only had eighteen rooms. After the war, but before it was damaged to the point of destruction by the earthquake of 1886, it served a tenement apartment building for lower-class blacks. One of these tenants, an elderly washer-woman went to the nearby well to get some water after a long day of toil. After raising the bucket full of water, a sigh behind her made her drop the bucket, but she managed to gather in the rope and raise the bucket again. As she started up the steps to her apartment, the bucket was taken from her and made the rounds to each patient in the former ward. All the while no living hands or lips touched the bucket. The old woman refused to take the offered bucket back and the other tenant found her cowering at the doorway, with an empty bucket at her side. In addition to buckets that make the rounds by themselves, the former hospital was also known to be troubled by men's voices and laughter from empty rooms and heavy footsteps on vacant stairs.

Another tale told about Trapman Street Hospital concerns a young lady of the evening who was at loose ends one evening when she was approached by a wounded man seeking water or morphine. Having no morphine but having a cracked pitcher, she gave the wounded man water... until he vanished from her arms, leaving an undamaged pitcher with a lip of silver. The story of the Army of the Dead, told above in connection with Mount Pleasant, is also told about the dead end streets near the hospital, which is actually a more fitting place.

The Gray Host

Ashepoo is a small rural community on the Ashepoo River in Colleton County between Jacksonboro and Green Pond just off US Highway 17. It used to be known as Ashepoo Junction and was on the Charleston and Savannah Railroad, which eventually became part of the Seaboard Coast Line. This route was heavily traveled by troop trains taking soldiers from the Upcountry to Charleston and surrounding areas. The troops were raucous and brave and had a merry time passing through Ashepoo. Many, being young and away from home for the first time, indulged in card games and drinking. In the mid-1960s, a witness reported walking down Main Street in February after work and encountering these same troops making their way to their destiny. He heard a train whistle followed by the sound of men singing. After another few moments he heard laughter and the hiss of a steam engine. Then all was quiet again. No train had passed by, at least not in this world.

Sadly, as good as this tale is, and as much as I hate to say Nancy Roberts (one of my inspirations) may have nodded, it is a mis-interpretation of a story contained in Part 4 of the South Carolina volume of the Slave Narratives gathered in the late 1930s by the Works Progress Administration during the New Deal. The narrator was an eighty year old ex-slave named William Rose. The events described likely would have occurred in 1862 or 1863. Rose describes an actual troop train, not a haunting. I can only assume the sighting in the mid-60s may have been a confusion dates, sadly.

Will the REAL Gray Man PLEASE Stand Up?

The Gray Man of Pawleys Island is probably the best known ghost in South Carolina and his tale is oft-told. He has appeared since 1822. Lucky tourists and residents of Pawleys have reported either seeing a figure dressed in gray on the beach or being approached by him just before a major tropic storm passes over. Those lucky enough to encounter him come through the storm unharmed or with minimal damage to their property. However, the living identity of the Gray Man has eluded researchers for decades, though sightings have been reported before major storms in 1822 (a hurricane that killed 300), 1893 (the Sea Island Hurricane that killed 1500 people), 1954 (Hurricane Hazel) and 1989 (Hurricane Hugo). Here are the three candidates. First we have the first settler and namesake of the island—Percival Pawley. His sons inherited his large land grant after his death about 1748. However, though his sons were very civic-minded, sponsoring Chapels of Ease and buying town lots in Georgetown, there is little record than Percival saw his land grant as anything more than an investment.

Secondly, we have the love interest of an island lass returning from a clash with the Indians. He rode on horseback up the coast from Georgetown to Pawleys Island. In his haste, he took a short cut through the marsh and horse and rider both tumbled into quicksand to their doom. The heartbroken young lady paced the beach for weeks seeking news of her love. Accounts vary on whether or not the couple was engaged or already married. After a few months, rumors of a large storm reached Pawleys. The girl's father decided not to evacuate due to some pressing business. A day or two before landfall, while she was one the beach, the young lady saw her love approach. He warned to her and her family to leave the island right away and immediately vanished. Upon hearing the story, the girl and her parents fled inland and avoided a horrible storm with no damage to their property. Another version of this story makes the man an unsuitable suitor for the daughter of a major rice planter from Charleston who had been sent away to Europe. The girl was told her lover had been killed in a duel and she then married her father's choice of husband. She and her husband honeymooned at Pawleys. The young man had turned to the sea to heal his broken heart and by some uncanny stroke of luck was shipwrecked off Pawleys Island and rescued by a servant of the husband. Learning the identity of his nurse, the man fled inland and died of an undetermined fever. The next year, he returned from the grave to warn his lover to flee her Pawleys Island retreat just before a storm hit, vanishing before the eyes of both her and her husband.

The final candidate for being the most famous ghost is South Carolina is Plowden Charles Jeannerette Weston, Lieutenant Governor of South Carolina under Milledge Luke Bonham and company commander of the Georgetown Rifle Guards, a home guard unit. He was also the builder of the Pelican Inn, which is also haunted. Plowden Weston was also the owner of Hagley Plantation, which we will visit shortly. Mr. Weston was also a historian and powerful orator. His love for the island was only rivaled by his love for his wife Emily and his plantation. The biggest difficulty with naming Plowden Weston as the Gray Man is the fact that the first reported appearance was in 1822 when Plowden was just two years old.

The Pelican Inn is also haunted by a Lady in Gray, who some witnesses think is Emily Plowden. She appears in a dress of gray gingham with pearl button and a white apron. She has been seen in the kitchen, and on the staircase going towards the bedrooms. Other witnesses think she could be a cousin of Emily and Plowden Weston, Mrs. William Mazyck, who inherited the Pelican Inn after the deaths of the Westons. The other ghosts reported at the Pelican Inn are two Boston Terriers that have been seen playing in the surf and on the beach in front of the house at dusk, only to vanish after a few seconds, leaving just tracks in the sand.

Hagley Landing

Hagley Landing is located on the Waccamaw River and is on property that once made up Hagley Plantation, the pride and joy of Plowden C.J. Weston mentioned above in connection with the legend of the Gray Man of Pawleys Island. Plowden Weston, as far as I know, is not one of the ghosts that haunt the Landing, however. That sad tale is something that would make Margaret Mitchell or Eudora Welty proud, but that I doubt any self-respecting editor would allow to see print. The story begins as so many do, with a wedding towards the end of the Civil War. The wedding was held at the plantation chapel, now sadly dismantled and scattered to the ends of Georgetown County, but the stained glass windows did survive and were given to Prince George Winyah Episcopal Church in Georgetown. A young bride married a dashing young swain and all was happiness. The wedding party retired to the landing to head off on their honeymoon and to accept the congratulations of the gather throng. Until a Confederate soldier in a ragged uniform rode up on a horse worn past all endurance and confronted the bride. The bride broke down; crying that she thought the soldier had been killed in battle. The solider then promised to interfere with the couple's happiness and leapt from the dock into the river, which was rapidly flowing out with the tide. The bride and groom then followed, one after the other. The first account of the haunting at Hagley dates from 1918 when a young man, waiting for his girlfriend to arrive via motor launch from Georgetown so they could attend a party on Pawleys Island. He saw the three unhappy suicides strolling down the road towards the landing. When he tried to speak, all three faded away as suddenly as they appeared. There have been reports of the figures being seen since, always dark and misty nights. The former Hagley Plantation is now a subdivision and the old landing is now a public boat dock for accessing the Waccamaw River, but the road leading to it is well-paved. I have sat there several times when conditions were right, but I have not been lucky…yet.

The USS Harvest Moon in Winyah Bay

The *USS Harvest Moon* had a brief but exciting career as a United States naval vessel. She was put in service on February 12, 1864, and immediately sent to Charleston to serve as a member of the South Atlantic Blockading Squadron, intercepting and deterring blockade runners from approaching Charleston and Georgetown. On February 26, 1864, Rear Admiral John Dahlgren made the *Harvest Moon* his flagship and it served from Tybee Island Georgia to Charleston Harbor. Admiral Dahlgren served as the commander of the Washington Navy Yard and head of Naval Ordinance during the Civil War for the Union. His best known achievement was the invention, in 1847, of the smooth-bore naval cannon named for him. While steaming out of Winyah Bay on March 1, 1865, bound for Charleston, the *Harvest Moon* hit a floating keg torpedo mine manufactured by Captain Thomas Daggett of Georgetown in his capacity as head of coastal defense from Little River to Georgetown and

Admiral John Dahlgren—The Union Admiral escaped the sinking of the *Harvest Moon* in Winyah Bay, but is the wreck still haunted?

sunk in about fifteen feet of water. Georgetown, one of the last ports open to the Confederacy had fallen on February 25th. Admiral Dahlgren narrowly missed being killed when a nearby bulkhead failed, but only one life was lost (John Hazzard, a wardroom steward was the unlucky sailor) and the crew moved to another vessel. The *Harvest Moon* was stripped of all machinery over the next month and remains embedded in the muddy bottom of the Bay to this day, her smokestack visible at low tide. Attempts to raise the vessel in 1963 failed due to unexplained equipment failures. Fishermen have reported hearing a low unearthly moan coming from the wreck during moonlit nights in the summer. Strangely, the moan is not blamed on the late Mr., Hazzard, but on a young African-American local stowaway killed in the explosion. Apparently, local tradition maintains that broken crockery must be placed inside the smokestack in order to keep the stowaway at peace.

Haunts in Georgetown — The Heriot and Morgan Houses

Georgetown is the county seat of Georgetown County and has been in existence since 1729. In the antebellum period the county and surrounding area produced about half the rice grown in the United States and the city was the largest rice-exporting port in the world. Most of the original homes still stand in the Historic District, and Georgetown is a contender for being one of the most haunted spots in South Carolina. Two of the homes in the Historic District claim to have ghosts dating from the Civil War period. These are the Heriot House and the Morgan House.

The Heriot House (also known as the Heriot-Tarbox House) is located on Cannon Street and was built by a man named Fyffe before the Revolution. Due to his loyalty to the Crown, the house was seized and he never recovered it. A later female owner used the garden to rendezvous with a Northern sea captain for years until the man stopped coming just before the outbreak of the Civil War. She would light a lamp in one of the third floor dormer windows that was visible from Winyah Bay when they could meet. Later, she used this same signal to assist blockade runners avoid capture by the Squadron just off the coast. After the War, she passed away alone except for her dogs. Later owners reported seeing lights in the dormer window while they were outside the house, but no light being present upon investigating, as well as hearing the click of several dog's claws on hardwood floors, even when no dogs were in the house. There have also been reports of the lady and her sea captain strolling along the waterfront in Georgetown.

The Morgan House (also known as the Morgan-Ginsler House) was built in 1825. After the outbreak of war, the owners fled and the house was used as a hospital for Union soldiers. Surgery was performed on the large dining table in the formal dining room. After the war, the Morgans returned to their home and began to experience crashes, bangs, moans and groans, and the sounds of moving furniture coming from the dining room. Upon investigation, nothing would be damaged in the quiet and empty room. Reports claim that the noises are still experienced. The house is located at 500 Prince Street.

The Battle of Honey Hill — Still Rages On

The Battle of Honey Hill was a minor battle during Sherman's March to the Sea from Atlanta, fought November 30, 1864. It did not involve Sherman's main force, but was a failed Union expedition under Maj. Gen. John Hatch that attempted to cut off the Charleston and Savannah Railroad in support of Sherman's projected arrival in Savannah. Hatch's expeditionary force left Hilton Head for Boyd's Neck near Beaufort on November 28. It consisted of five thousand men. They steamed up the Broad River in transports to cut the Charleston and Savannah Railroad near Pocotaligo. Due to a heavy fog the troops were not disembarked from the transports until late the following afternoon, and Hatch immediately started forward to cut the railroad near the community of Grahamville, now located in Jasper County. Hatch was misled by unfaithful guides and outdated and error-filled maps and was unable to proceed on the right road until the morning of November 30. At Honey Hill, a few miles from Grahamville, he encountered a force of regulars and militia under Confederate Colonel Charles Colcock, with a battery of seven guns across the road. Determined attacks were launched by United States Colored Troops, including the famed 54th and 55th Massachusetts Regiments. The position of the Federal force was such that only one section of artillery could be used at a time and the Confederates were too well entrenched to be dislodged. Union First Lieutenant Orson Bennett was awarded for saving three Union cannons from capture in front of enemy lines. Fighting kept up until dark when Hatch, realizing that he could not turn the flank of the enemy, withdrew to his transports

Enslaved Black people — Slavery, and either its protection or demise, was the primary cause of the Civil War.

and returned to Hilton Head, having lost 89 men killed, 629 wounded, and 28 missing. The Confederate casualties amounted to 8 killed and 39 wounded. After the war, General Hatch was the military commander of Charleston for six months in 1865. The exact site of the battle is not public knowledge due to its sensitivity as an archaeological site and possible targets for relic seekers. It is on the National Register of Historic Places as of July 4, 2004. Please be respectful in the event you do locate the site as it is a true national treasure and the resting place of several soldiers as well. Of course, since the site is private property, please do not trespass. In any event, the reported haunting is centered near the surviving Confederate earthworks (wrongly identified as a fort in one of the sources I found). On certain nights from late November to mid-January the sounds of both cannon and small arms fire has been heard in the surrounding woods as have the screams of men fighting. When the area is approached, silence falls like a blanket over the area. Given that Honey

Hill was one of the last victories enjoyed by the Confederate Army, I am not at all surprised that the battle is still being fought.

The Land's End Light

Saint Helena Island was witness to one of the few Union successes early in the Civil War. Port Royal Sound was the scene of a Union victory in November 1861 when a combined force of regular Army and Naval vessels captured Forts Walker and Beauregard on nearby islands, leading to the near-desertion of Hilton Head and Beaufort by the planters and setting the stage for one of the grandest social engineering experiments of the war, the Port Royal Experiment. The Port Royal Experiment was a program begun during the Civil War in which former slaves successfully worked on the land of some fifty plantations abandoned by the white owners. Several private Northern charity organizations stepped in to help the former slaves become self-sufficient. The freedmen demonstrated their ability to work the land efficiently and live independently of white control. They assigned themselves daily tasks for cotton growing and spent their extra time fishing, hunting, and cultivating their own crops. By selling their surplus crops, the locals acquired small amounts of property. In 1865, President Andrew Johnson ended the experiment, returning the land to its previous white owners.

The Land's End Light has accumulated almost as many versions as there are witnesses over the last hundred-plus years. First we will address what all the tales have in common. In Frogmore, off US Highway 21, you turn down Land's End Road towards Penn Center and pass the ruined Chapel of Ease (which has ghost stories of its own to tell) and you will reach a straight stretch of highway on the southern end of Saint Helena Island near the remains of the Spanish-American War era Fort Fremont. A particularly good spot is near Adam Street Baptist Church. Simply park your car and wait. An oval yellowish-orange light about ten feet above the pavement will approach. One other point of agreement. There are no railroad tracks on the island, so you can rule that out as a possible source of the story and as a source of false reports as well. Now for the differences of opinion, which are legion. Some say the Light will approach a parked car and vanish, others that it will hover nearby. Others say the Light will pass speeding cars. According to reports, at least two drivers have died chasing the Light, hence my advice to stay put. There are five different possible origins for the Light. The first states that it is the lantern of a Confederate sentry murdered and beheaded by Yankee troops in late 1861. The head was thrown into Port Royal Sound and the body left to rot. Since then, the poor solider seeks his head, using his iron lantern to light his way. The second version claims that the unlucky solider was a member of the occupying Union Army who was robbed and murdered after a card game. The third legend claims that the Light belongs to a slave seeking his wife after he was sold down the river before the Civil War. Version number four claims the Light is the spirit of a soldier from Fort Fremont killed by civilians from Beaufort in a brawl in 1910. The final and most recent version claims that the Light is the headlight of a school bus that wrecked near a certain oak tree under a full moon. The Light is the headlight of the bus and when seen it is accompanied by the screams of the terrified children as the Light (and bus) goes off the road to their doom. The more practical witnesses blame marsh gas, static electricity, or an optical illusion caused by the road. Another light has been seen near Frogmore Manor. This is claimed to be the glow of a lantern hung on an upstairs porch to guide blockade runners seeking entry to safe waters.

I have been lucky enough to see the Land's End Light twice. I went on two different occasions and parked in the "designated" area along with three or four other cars. We waited until just after dark and were treated to a faint orange blob of light higher than my six foot two coming down the center of the road. As it got to within about twenty feet of us, it simply vanished as quickly as it appeared. No traffic marred the display and no one was playing with a flashlight that I could see, not that I saw the tell-tale beam from a spotlight or flashlight. The light came, approached and vanished within about five minutes. I definitely recommend the trip, and check out Penn Center and the other historic spots on the Island as well.

The Lucas Bay Light — Horry County

The story of the haunting at the old bridge on Lucas Bay Road is an excellent example of the terror Sherman's approach generated among those thought to be in his path. After Sherman reached Savannah just before Christmas 1864, everyone knew that South Carolina would soon suffer the same fate as much of eastern Georgia, if not far worse. Among those frightened and unsure was a young mother living in the community of Lucas Bay, near the Great Pee Dee River in Horry County. Having heard a rumor that Sherman was approaching Georgetown, a scant thirty miles away, the mother decided to hide the thing she held most dear, her infant child, under the small bridge over a canal at a nearby rice field. Just before dark, a thunderstorm came over, sparking a downpour. The mother, suddenly realizing the danger, dashed to the bridge to retrieve her child. Sadly, she fell, hit her head and was drowned, followed by her sleeping child. Years later, long after the mother and child were forgotten, a small red light began to appear on Lucas Bay Road near the old bridge. It was about the size of the end of a lit cigar, grew to about the size of a child's balloon and then vanished. Locals claim that rainy nights just after dusk when other lights are absent are prime viewing times. Some have claimed to hear a baby wailing when the light appears, but not everyone experiences both phenomena. Indeed, like other most ghost lights, some may see it and some may not during the same visit. However, according to an online source, the South Carolina Department of Transportation did some major work in the Lucas Bay area about 1996 or so. Sightings of the light have dropped dramatically since. I have visited Lucas Bay three different times trying to find the light without any luck. Of course, I first learned about the light in 2000, which is the way things go sometimes.

Otter Island — Fort Drayton

Otter Island is located between Edisto and Saint Helena Islands on the South Carolina coast. It is currently uninhabited and is a wildlife preserve. Confederate forces constructed the fort on Otter Island in 1861, but quickly abandoned it when Federal troops captured Port Royal in November 1861. It was a triangular fortification with two sides facing St Helena Sound and a ditch surrounding it. After the Federal occupation of Port Royal, free slaves began to congregate on Otter Island. Federal reconnaissance of the fort noted its importance in the control of entrances to the Ashepoo and South Edisto Rivers. Subsequently, the Federals established a permanent fortification there for the remainder of the war. The Federal force renamed it Fort Drayton and occupied it beginning in mid-December 1861. To ease communication between Hilton Head Island and Folly Island, a network of signal towers was constructed on the coast, one on Otter Island near the fort. Fort Drayton was named for Captain Percival Drayton, who was born in Charleston, moved to Philadelphia as a child and served in the United States Navy during the Civil War. He commanded the naval portion of the force that captured Port Royal Sound in November 1861 and also fought with Admiral David Farragut at Mobile Bay. His older brother Thomas Drayton commanded the Confederate troops at Forts Walker and Beauregard. His defeat at Port Royal did not dim his star, as served as a Brigadier General in Virginia until 1863. He served in the western theater of the war until 1865. According to local legend, Otter Island also served as a makeshift prisoner-of-war camp, though most of the troops and their servants held there were locals and escaped fairly easily. Prior to the Civil War, during the British occupation of the Lowcountry during the Revolution, Otter Island was used to hold slaves intended to be shipped to Jamaica or Barbados or other colonies. Those who were not shipped overseas were left to die on the island. The legend continues that the captives still cry out for help or rescue and that the unwary may be grabbed and pulled ashore if they get too close.

I have not yet visited Otter Island, as the island is only accessible by boat. But given the fact that it is open to overnight camping six months out of the year, I may be grabbing my hammock and renting a kayak very soon. And yes, I will hug the shoreline on the Otter Island side when I approach.

Works Cited

ARTICLES

Boyanoski, John. "Upstate Rich With Legends of Ghosts and Haunted Buildings." Greenville News. October 29, 2003.

Boykin, Hope. "Plantations in Lower Kershaw County: Part I." Names in South Carolina. Volume XVI (Winter 1969), 45-8.

"Halloween in Union County." Union Grapevine, October 2004.

Haynesworth, James. "Place Names near Hagood." Names in South Carolina. Volume XIII (November 1966), 27-8.

Hendricks, Dave. "Spooky Fort Guards Lands End" (Ft. Fremont). Beaufort Gazette. October 31, 2000. 3C.

Kemp, Kristina. "Buildings Inhabited By Ghosts?" Daily Gamecock, October 31, 2006.

Knauss, Christina. "Columbia's Historic Haunts." The State, October 27, 2000.

Lee, Eddie. Things That Go Bump in the Dark. York County Magazine (Rock Hill, SC, Pluto Publishing) v.8, issue 10 (October 2011), 32, 54.

"Madeline—The Legend." Newberry College... Where People Make It Special (Newberry SC, Newberry College. October 29, 1986.

Nutt, Karen. "Upstate Has Share of Ghosts, Goblins." Spartanburg Herald-Journal. October 27, 1994.

Patterson, Lezlie. "Ghost Town." The State, July 22, 2006.

Poucher, Dean. "The Ghost of Land's End." Savannah News-Press. November 10, 1974, A1.

Rupon, Kristy Eppley. "Camden's Spirits of the Past." The State, October 30, 2003.

Self, Jamie. York's Haunted Hotel. The (Rock Hill, SC) Herald. October 31, 2011, A1.

Shannon, James. "The Haunting of the Upstate." Greenville (SC) MetroBEAT. October 20, 2004.

Spieler, Gerhard. "Ghosts, Past and Present." Beaufort Gazette. August 5, 1980, 6A.

Spieler, Gerhard. "Land's End Light— Real or Imaginary?" Beaufort Gazette. June 20, 1974, A1.

Stone, Phillip. Are there ghosts at Wofford? Old Gold and Black (Spartanburg, SC, Wofford College). November 1, 1991,1.

BOOKS

Asfar, Dan and Edrick Thay. Ghost Stories of the Civil War. Auburn WA: Ghost House, 2003.Asfar, Dan. Haunted Battlefields. Edmonton, Alberta: Ghost House Books, 2004.

Baptist, Edward. Creating an Old South: Middle Florida's Plantation Frontier Before the Civil War. Chapel Hill NC: UNC Press, 2002.

Barrett, John. Sherman's March through the Carolinas. Chapel Hill NC, UNCP, 1956.

Bennett, John. The Doctor to the Dead: Grotesque Legends and Folk Tales of Old Charleston. New York: Rinehart, 1946.

Bolick, Julian. The Return of the Gray Man and Georgetown Ghosts. Georgetown SC: Jacobs Brothers, 1956.

Bostick, Douglas. Sunken Plantations: The Santee Cooper Project. Charleston: The History Press, 2008.

Bostick, Douglas. The Union Is Dissolved!, Charleston and Fort Sumter in the Civil War. Charleston, SC: The History Press, 2009.

Botkin, BA. A Civil War Treasury of Tales, Legends and Folklore. New York, Random House, 1960.

Boyanoski, John. Ghosts of Upstate South Carolina. Mountville, PA: Shelor and Son, 2006.

Boyanoski, John. More Ghosts of Upstate South Carolina. Mountville, PA: Shelor and Son, 2008.

Brennan, Patrick. Secessionville: Assault on Charleston. Campbell, CA: Savas Publishing, 1996.

Brown, Alan. Stories From the Haunted South. Jackson, MS: University of Mississippi Press, 2004.

Burton, E.M. The Siege of Charleston, 1861-1865. Columbia, SC: USC Press, 1970.

Buxton, Geordie and Ed Macy. Haunted Harbor: Charleston's Maritime Ghosts and the Unexplained. Charleston: The History Press, 2005.

Capers, Ellison. Confederate Military History, v. 5: South Carolina. Series editor, Clement Evans. Secacus, NJ: Blue and Gray Press (Book Sales, Inc), 1976.

Carmichael, Sherman. Forgotten Tales of South Carolina. Charleston, SC: The History Press, 2011.

Catawba Regional Planning Commission. Historic Sites Survey: Chester County. No Publisher Data, 1976.

Catawba Regional Planning Commission. Historic Sites Survey: Union County. No Publisher Data, 1976.

Catawba Regional Planning Commission. Historic Sites Survey: York County. No Publisher Data, 1976.

Cauthen, Charles. South Carolina Goes to War, 1860-1865. Columbia SC: USC Press, 2005.

Civil War Preservation Trust. Civil War Sites: The Official Guide to Battlefields, Monuments and More. Guilford, CT: Globe Pequot, 2003.

Collins, Anne. A Goodly Heritage: History of Chester County, South Carolina. Columbia, SC: R.L. Bryan, 1986.

Cromie, Alice. A Tour Guide to the Civil War: The Complete State-by-State Guide to Battlegrounds, Landmarks, Museums, Relics, and Sites. Nashville, Rutledge Hill, 1992.

Cross, J. Russell. Historic Ramblin's Through Berkeley. Columbia: RL Bryan, 1985.

D'Arcy, David. Civil War Tour of Charleston. Atglen, PA: Schiffer Publishing, 2010.

Davis, Burke. Sherman's March. New York, Random House, 1980.

Edgar, Walter (editor). The South Carolina Encyclopedia. Columbia: USC Press, 2006.

Edgar, Walter. South Carolina: A History. Columbia, SC: USCP, 1998.

Floyd, Blanche. Tales along the Grand Strand of South Carolina. Winston-Salem, NC: Bandit Books, 1996.

Floyd, Blanche. Tales along the Kings Highway of South Carolina. Winston-Salem, NC: Bandit Books, 1999.

Floyd, E. Randall. Great Southern Mysteries. New York: Barnes and Noble, 2000.

Floyd, E. Randall. In the Realm of Ghosts and Hauntings: 40 Supernatural Occurrences From Across the World. New York: Barnes and Noble, 2002.

Fox, William Price. South Carolina Off the Beaten Path. Old Saybrook, CT: Pequot Press, 1996.

Freeman, Douglas Southall. R.E. Lee: A Biography. Volume Four. New York: Scribner's, 1935.

Gibbes, James. Who Burnt Columbia?. Newberry, SC: Elbert H. Aull Company, 1902.

Gragg, Rod. Pirates, Planters, and Patriots: Historical Tales from the Grand Strand. Winston-Salem, NC: Peace Hill, 1984.

Graydon, Nell. South Carolina Ghost Tales. Beaufort SC: Beaufort Book Company, 1969.

Graydon, Nell. Tales of Beaufort. Orangeburg, SC: Sandlapper Publishing, 2006.

Graydon, Nell. Tales of Columbia. Columbia: RL Bryan, 1964.

Graydon, Nell. Tales of Edisto. Orangeburg, SC: Sandlapper Publishing, 2000.

Gregorie, Anne. History of Sumter County South Carolina. Sumter SC: Library Board of Sumter County, 1954.

Griffin, John. A Pictorial History of the Confederacy. Jefferson, NC: McFarland and Company, 2004.

Hall, Lynne. South Carolina Ghosts: They Are Among Us. Raleigh: Sweetwater Press, 2006.

Hall, Lynne. Strange but True South Carolina. N.p.: Sweetwater Press, 2007.

Harwell, Richard and Philip Racine. The Fiery Trail: A Union Officer's Account of Sherman's Last Campaign. Knoxville, U of Tennessee Press, 1986.

Hauck, Dennis. Haunted Places: The National Directory: Ghostly Abodes, Sacred Sites, UFO Landings, and Other Supernatural Locations. New York: Penguin, 2002.

Henning, Helen (editor). Columbia: Capital City of South Carolina, 1786-1936. Columbia: RL Bryan, 1936.

Hicks, Brian and Schuyler Krope. Raising the Hunley: The Remarkable

History and Recovery of the Lost Confederate Submarine. Knew York, Ballentine, 2002.

Hollis, Daniel Walker. University of South Carolina. Volume I: College to University. Columbia: USC Press, 1956.

Howard, Blair. Battlefields of the Civil War: A Guide for Travelers. V.2. Edison, NJ: Hunter Publishing, 1995.

Hunt, John and Joan Faunt. South Carolina Secedes. Columbia, SC: USC Press, 1960.

Huntsinger, Elizabeth. Ghosts of Georgetown. Winston-Salem: John F. Blair, 1995.

Huntsinger, Elizabeth. More Ghosts of Georgetown. Winston-Salem: John F. Blair, 1998.

Isenberg, Nancy and Andrew Burstein, editors. Mortal Remains: Death in Early America. Philadelphia: U of Pennsylvania, 2003.

Johnson, Clint. Touring the Carolinas' Civil War Sites. Winston-Salem: John F. Blair, 1996.

Johnson, Tally. Ghosts of the Pee Dee. Charleston: The History Press, 2009.

Johnson, Tally. Ghosts of the South Carolina Midlands. Charleston: The History Press, 2007.

Johnson, Tally. Ghosts of the South Carolina Upcountry. Charleston: The History Press, 2005.

Jones, Katharine. When Sherman Came: Southern Women and the "Great March." Indianapolis: Bobbs-Merrill, 1964.

Julien, Carl. Beneath So Kind a Sky: The Scenic and Architectural Beauty of South Carolina. Columbia: USC Press, 1948.

Kirkland, Thomas and Robert Kennedy. Historic Camden: Part Two, Nineteenth Century. Columbia: The State Company, 1926.

Lachicotte, Alberta. Georgetown Rice Plantations. Columbia, SC: The State Commercial Printing, 1955.

Lathan, Robert. History of Hopewell Associate Reformed Presbyterian Church, Chester County, SC, Together with Biographical Sketches of its Four Pastors. York(ville), SC: Steam Presses of the Yorkville Enquirer, 1879.

Lee, J. Edward and Ron Chepesiuk. South Carolina in the Civil War: The Confederate Experience in Letters and Diaries. Jefferson, NC: McFarland and Company, 2000.

Leiding, Harriette. Historic Houses of South Carolina. Spartanburg, SC: The Reprint Company, 1975.

Lucas, Marion. Sherman and the Burning of Columbia. Columbia, SC: USCP, 2000.

Mackintosh, Robert (Jr.)., comp. and ed. "Dear Martha...": The Confederate War Letters of a South Carolina Soldier, Alexander Faulkner Fewell. Columbia, SC: RL Bryan, 1976.

Macy, Edward and Julian Buxton III. The Ghosts of Charleston. New York: Beaufort Books, 2001.

Manley, Roger. Weird Carolinas. New York: Sterling, 2007.

Meredith, Roy. Storm Over Sumter: The Opening Engagement of the Civil War. New York: Simon and Schuster, 1957.

Miers, Earl, ed. When the World Ended: The Diary of Emma LeConte. New York: Oxford UP, 1957.

No Author Given. The Scrapbook: A Compilation of Historical Facts About Places and Events in Laurens County South Carolina. Laurens SC: Laurens County Historical Society and Laurens County Arts Council, 1982.

Orr, Bruce. Ghosts of Berkeley County, South Carolina. Charleston, SC: The History Press, 2011.

Profit, Jason. Haunted Greenville, South Carolina. Charleston, SC: The History Press, 2011.

Ravenel, Mrs. St. Julien. Charleston: The Place and the People. New York: McMillan, 1912.

Roberts, Nancy. Civil War Ghost Stories and Legends. Columbia, SC: USouthCarolinaP, 1993.

Roberts, Nancy. Ghosts from the Coast. Chapel Hill, NC: UNC Press, 2000.

Roberts, Nancy. The Haunted South: Where Ghosts Still Roam. Columbia: USC Press, 1995.

Roberts, Nancy. South Carolina Ghosts: From the Coast to the Mountains. Columbia: USC Press, 1983.

Rogers, George (Jr.). History of Georgetown County South Carolina. Columbia, SC: USC Press, 1970.

Rhyne, Nancy. Coastal Ghosts: Haunted Places From Wilmington, North Carolina to Savannah, Georgia. Orangeburg SC: Sandlapper, 2005.

Rhyne, Nancy. Touring the Coastal South Carolina Backroads. Winston-Salem, NC: John F. Blair, 1996.

Schlosser, S.E. . Spooky South Carolina: Tales of Hauntings, Strange Happenings, and Other Local Lore. Guilford, CT: Globe Pequot Press, 2011.

Simons, Jane. A Guide to Columbia, South Carolina's Capital City. Columbia: RL Bryan, 1945.

Smith, Steven. Whom We Would Never More See: History and Archaeology Recover the Lives and Deaths of African-American Civil War Soldiers on Folly Island, South Carolina. Columbia: SCDAH, 1993.

Spaeth, Frank, ed.. Phantom Army of the Civil War and Other Southern Ghost Stories. St. Paul, MN: Llewellyn Publications, 1997.

State Historic Preservation Office. African American Historic Places in South Carolina. Columbia: SCDAH, 2009.

Sumter, John. Some Old Stateburg Homes and the Church of the Holy Cross. Sumter, SC: Sumter Printing, 1949.

Sumter, Thomas. Stateburg and Its People. Sumter, SC: Sumter Printing, 1949.

Swanberg, WA. First Blood: The Story of Fort Sumter. New York, Scribner's, 1957.

Symonds, Craig. A Battlefield Atlas of the Civil War. Annapolis, MD: Nautical and Aviation Publishing Company of America, 1983.

Taylor, Troy. Field Guide to Haunted Graveyards: A Research Guide to Investigating America's Haunted Cemeteries. Alton, IL: Whitechapel Productions Press, 2003.

Testimony Taken by the Joint Select Committee to Inquire into the Condition of Affairs in the Late Insurrectionary States. South Carolina. Volume II. Washington: Government Printing Office, 1872.

Todd, Caroline and Sidney Wait. South Carolina: A Day at a Time. Orangeburg, SC: Sandlapper Publishing, 2008.

Vandiver, Louise. Traditions and History of Anderson County. Atlanta: Ruralist Press, 1928.

Wise, Stephen. Gate of Hell: Campaign for Charleston Harbor, 1863. Columbia, SC: USC Press, 1994.

Woodward, C. Vann, ed.. Mary Chestnut's Civil War. New Haven, CT: Yale UP, 1981.

Woodward, C. Vann and Elisabeth Muhlenfeld. The Private Mary Chestnut: The Unpublished Civil War Diaries. New York: Oxford UP, 1984.

Workers of the Writers Program of the Works Progress Administration in the State of South Carolina. South Carolina: A Guide to the Palmetto

State. New York: Oxford University Press, 1941.

Workers of the Writers Program of the Works Progress Administration in the State of South Carolina. South Carolina Folk Tales: Stories of Animals and Supernatural Beings. Columbia: South Carolina Education Association, no date.

Zepke, Terrance. Best Ghost Tales of South Carolina. Sarasota, FL: Pineapple Press, 2004.

PAMPHLETS

Brown, Robert. Sumter, South Carolina; Last Days; Potter's Raid and the Civil War. Sumter SC: Sumter Convention and Visitors Bureau, 2005.

Gottshall, Thomas. First Presbyterian Churchyard Columbia, South Carolina. Columbia: First Presbyterian Church, no date.

Historic Greenville Foundation and City of Greenville Parks and Recreation. Springwood Cemetery: A Historical Tour. N.p. N.d.

No Author Given. South Carolina State House Guide. Columbia: SC Department of Parks, Recreation and Tourism, No date.

No Author Given. Quaker Cemetery. Camden, SC: No publisher given, no date.

Olde English District. Civil War Sites: Your Guide to the Civil War Sites in South Carolina's Olde English District, Chester, Chesterfield, Fairfield, Kershaw, Lancaster, Union, and York Counties. Chester SC: Olde English Tourism Commission, 2009.

State House Tour Service. A Walk through History: The Grounds of the South Carolina State House. Columbia: SC Department of Parks, Recreation and Tourism, no date.

WEBSITES

32 Legare Street Sword Gate House. http://www.preservationsociety.

org/program_historicmarkers-Detail.asp?hmID=31

ACE Basin-Cultural Resources. http://nerrs.noaa.gov/Doc/SiteProfile/ACEBasin/html/cultural/cultres/crstfile.htm

Beauregard-Keyes House New Orleans, Louisiana. http://www.graveaddiction.com/bkeyes.html

The Battle of Honey Hill by Kathy Dhalle. http://www.bitsofblueandgray.com/Feb2_2.htm

Battle of Port Royal, 7 November 1861. http://www.historyofwar.org/articles/battles_port_royal.html

Civil War Battles in South Carolina. http://www.civilwaracademy.com/civil-war-battles-in-south-carolina.html

Civil War Sites in South Carolina. http://cr.nps.gov/hps/abpp/battles/SCmap.htm

Florena Budwin. http://home.att.net/~florencestockade/florena.htm

Fort Moultrie National Monument.http://www.nps.gov/fosu/history-culture/fort_moultrie.htm

Friends of the Hunley. http://www.hunley.org/main_index.asp?CONTENT=MISSION

The Ghost of Mordecai House. http://www.northcarolinaghosts.com/piedmont/mordecai.php

The Ghosts of Longstreet Theatre. http://www.examiner.com/article/the-ghosts-of-longstreet-theatre

The Haunted Fields of Andersonville. https://dalejyoung.com/the-haunted-fields-of-andersonville/

Haunted South Carolina. http://www.haunted-places.com/misc_states/HAUNT_SC.htm

Historical Background of Potter's Raid. http://pottersraid.tripod.com/

historicalbackground.html

Is There a Ghost in USC's Longstreet Theatre?http://www.discover-southcarolina.com/Insider/Arts_and_Culture/Blog/6430

Legare Street.http://www.ccpl.org/content.asp?id=15671&action=detail&catid=6025&parentid=5747

National Register of Historic Places- South Carolina. www.nationalregister.sc.gov

Overview. http://www.battleofaiken.org/Overview.html

Samuel McGowan: The Fifth Avenue Ghost. http://trrcobb.blogspot.com/2014/12/samuel-mcgowan-fifth-avenue-ghost.html

Scares and Haunts of Charleston. http://scaresandhauntsofcharleston.wordpress.com/

Seeks Ghosts: Haunted Andersonville Prison. https://seeksghosts.blogspot.com/2016/02/haunted-andersonville-prison.html

The Shadowlands- Haunted Places in South Carolina. http://www.theshadowlands.net/places/southcarolina.htm

South Carolina Campaign. http://www.rootsweb.ancestry.com/~orphanm/scarcamp.htm

South Carolina Historical Markers Associated With the Civil War. http://sc150civilwar.palmettohistory.org/civilwarhistoricmarkers.pdf

South Carolina Map of Battles American Civil War. http://americancivilwar.com/statepic/south_carolina.html

South Carolina Markers. http://www.hmdb.org//Results.asp?State=-South%20Carolina

South Carolina Plantations. http://south-carolina-plantations.com

The South Carolina Secessionist- Sherman's March Through South Carolina. http://www.researchonline.net/sccw/sher_03.htm

South Carolina Slave Narratives Volume XIV Part 4. https://archive.org/stream/SouthCarolinaNarrativesVolumeXIVPart4-slavery/South%20Carolina%20Narratives%2C%20Volume%20XIV%2C%20Part%204#page/n53/

Southern Spirit Guide: Haunted South Carolina. http://southernspiritguide.blogspot.com/search/label/South%20Carolina%20Ghosts

Talvande Mansion. http://www.hauntedhouses.com/states/sc/talvande_mansion.htm

Wateree to Kings Creek-(3 Segments)-Norfolk-Southern. http://www.abandonedrails.com/Wateree_to_Kings_Creek

Weird Georgia The Scapegoat General's Spirit. http://www.brownsguides.com/blog/weird-georgia-the-scapegoat-generals-spirit/

About the Author

Mr. Johnson is a graduate of Spartanburg Methodist College and Wofford College with degrees in history. He is the author of *Ghosts of the South Carolina Upcountry*, *Ghosts of the South Carolina Midlands*, *Ghosts of the Pee Dee* (all for The History Press) and he also has a story in *An Improbable Truth: The Paranormal adventures of Sherlock Holmes* (from Mocha Memoirs Press). His newest full-length release is an anthology of Southern Gothic ghost fiction titled *Creek Walking* from Falstaff Books. He also has stories in two anthologies from Prospective Press. His tale "Bloody Bonnet at Blue Hole" was recently included on the Valentine Wolfe album Winternight Whisperings. Mr. Johnson was also the recipient of the first Caldwell Sims Award for Excellence in Southern Folklore from the USC-Union Upcountry Literary Festival. He is also the Storyteller-In-Residence for Palmetto State Hangers, a hammock camping group. Find him at http://tallyjohnson.wix.com/sc-ghost-talker and facebook.com/tallyjohnson3